Food for Thought

The Vegetarian Philosophy

Ananda Mitra

©1991 Ananda Marga Publications. Reprinted with permission by NUCLEUS Publications, Rt. 2, Box 49, Willow Springs, Missouri, U.S.A. 65793

Readers interested in learning more about yoga, meditation or the vegetarian philosophy may contact Ananda Marga Yoga of North America, 97-38 42nd Ave., Corona, NY 11368

TABLE OF CONTENTS

PART I: FOOD

THE SCIENCE OF YOGA

In spite of the tremendous achievements of modern civilization, today's human beings seem to be less tranquil and happy than ever before, for our lives have gone out of balance. Crowds and pollution, the rapid pace of life and the pressure of work, the lack of proper exercise, improper food and over-eating, negative influences surrounding us on all sides—all these degenerate our health and disturb our minds. Through the scientific practice of yoga we can learn to reestablish the balance of a natural life, to regain the radiant health of our bodies and the serenity of our minds and hearts.

This practice begins with the development of the physical body, for it is the vehicle on our journey towards our ultimate goal of infinite, blissful Consciousness. And as we develop our bodies, we must take special care of the foods we eat, for they have the most profound effect on all levels of our being—body, mind and spirit.

FOOD AND THE FORCES OF THE UNIVERSE

We are what we eat. Those delicious morsels of food we pop into our mouths eventually develop every cell of our bodies and affect not only our physical health, but the way we think as well. Recent experiments have shown that certain foods directly influence the workings of the brain by affecting the brain's chemical neurotransmitters which are involved in different mental and physical functions: in memory, sleep, motor coordination, pain, depression, learning ability, and even our perception of reality. Eating foods rich in lecithin, for instance (which is contained in soybeans) can increase our memory power; whereas eating a meal rich in carbohydrates and poor in proteins is the surest way to make the brain drowsy for hours afterwards.* Research has indicated that even the symptoms of schizophrenia, hyperactivity, and certain other mental disorders can be alleviated by corrective diet therapy.

Thousands of years ago, yoga sages realized the tremendous importance of the food we eat on the state of our bodies and minds. Through their deep, introspective investigations into the nature of the universe, those ancient yogis realized what modern

---

*Carbohydrates stimulate the production of insulin, which in turn increases the level of seratonin in the brain—which then makes us sleepy.

scientists since Einstein are just beginning to discover: that the entire manifested universe is composed of vibrations—vibrations of energy and, ultimately, vibrations of consciousness. In this universe of multifarious waves, what we call matter (solids, liquids and gases), sound, light, and thought, are all simply waves vibrating at different frequencies, from gross to subtle. All foods are also permeated with their own subtle vibrations, at different frequencies, and these vibrations in turn affect the body and mind of the person eating them. After long experimentation with different foods on their own bodies and minds (for the yogis were practical, empirical scientists, not merely theoreticians), those ancient seers characterized foods into three categories, corresponding to the three forces which are operating simultaneously everywhere in the universe, in all entities. When any one of these vibrational flows, or energy forces, predominates in any object or creature, it takes on the qualities of that force.

The sentient force & sentient foods

The first of these universal forces is the sentient force of self-awareness, love, peace, purity and joy. When the sentient force* is predominant in our minds, we feel peaceful, relaxed and calm, and our minds flow easily to higher levels of consciousness. Sentient foods are those in which the sentient force is dominant, which make our minds clear and calm. These foods are the basis of the yogic diet, for they are the most conducive to physical health and mental peace; they are the best diet for those who seek to elevate their minds to higher states of consciousness and attain self-realization.**

This group of foods includes fruits, most vegetables, beans and nuts, grains, milk and milk products, and moderate amounts of most herbs and spices. The sentient diet (sometimes called *lacto-vegetarian* because it includes milk and milk products) provides a wide variety of nutrients supplying proteins, carbohydrates, fats, and all the essential vitamins and minerals.

The mutative force & mutative foods

The second of these universal flows is the mutative force***, the

---

* *Sattvaguna* in Sanskrit.
** In fact, for those practising yoga postures (*asanas*), it is recommended that a sentient diet be taken to obtain the maximum benefit from these subtle exercises.
*** *Rajoguna* in Sanskrit.

force of restless movement, activity or change. When this force is predominant in our minds, we become agitated, nervous and restless, unable to calm down and relax. Mutative foods are those which stimulate the body and mind, and should be taken only in moderation in order to maintain our mental balance. Indeed, eating too much of these stimulating foods disturbs the mind and makes it impossible to still the mind for subtle mental pursuits such as meditation. Included in this category are: caffeinated beverages such as coffee and tea, carbonated drinks, chocolate, hot spices such as red peppers, fermented foods, and some medicinal drugs.

The static force and static foods

The third force is the static force*, the force of dullness, inertia, decay and death. Death occurs when the other two forces in any living entity have completely waned and the static force alone predominates. When this force is operating in our minds, we feel sleepy, dull and listless, lacking energy and initiative.

The static foods include meats, fish, onion, garlic, eggs, mushrooms, alcohol, cigarettes, drugs, and food that is fermented, stale or spoiled. These foods should be avoided by those who seek to attain health of body and elevation of mind. However, in certain situations, according to the climate or activity of an individual, they may be eaten—for instance, in extremely cold climates where meat or small quantities of alcoholic beverages may be necessary to maintain body heat.

Mushrooms

Some vegetarians consider mushrooms to be an alternate source of protein to replace meat. Indeed, mushrooms are high in protein but their over-all effect may be toxic to mind and body. Unlike other plants, which live by photosynthesis (deriving energy from the sun's light), mushrooms lack chlorophyl and thus cannot utilize the sun's energy. They must therefore take their nutrients from dead plants, animals, animals' feces, etc. Extracting their energy from death and darkness, they pass on these static qualities directly to their consumer. Even the most prized species of edible mushrooms are known to be difficult to digest if eaten in quantity,

---

* *Tamoguna* in Sanskrit.

inducing mental dullness, physical lethargy and drowsiness; for in many cases, the amount of energy needed to extract useful nutrients from mushrooms is more than the energy gained thereby. Mushrooms also decay very rapidly, producing highly toxic ptomaine alkaloids. Some edible field mushrooms picked on a warm day and stored without adequate ventilation may be entirely rotten by the time they are taken home. Thus many vegetarians avoid the fungus group as a good source, for all the elements needed to sustain our physical health can be obtained in a fresh sentient diet.

Onions & garlic
Many doctors contend that garlic and onions increase the acidity of the stomach, and can even cause or aggravate ulcers. Since over-acidity is one of the chief causes of disease, eating garlic or onions can be very harmful for health. Moreover, as these foods create much heat in the body, they are disturbing to the mind as well. Just as the fumes from onions and garlic irritate the tender tissues of the eye to produce tears, so they greatly agitate the mind, and are therefore avoided by those seeking to maintain mental peace or achieve higher consciousness.

Eggs
Eggs contain a high amount of fatty cholesterol which is one of the main causes of high blood pressure and heart disease. Every egg contains 200 mg of cholesterol, twice the amount in a 5 oz. steak! Thus many doctors advise their heart patients to avoid eggs entirely, and nutrition experts contend that all the benefits of a pure vegetarian diet can be completely negated by eating too many eggs!

WHAT'S WRONG WITH EATING MEAT?

The first thing many people ask when they hear about the vegetarian diet is, "What's wrong with eating meat? Millions of people do it; why should I stop?"

There are very important reasons why it is preferable not to eat meat—not emotional or sentimental, but very convincing and scientific reasons. If you consider these points carefully, certainly you will want to try a vegetarian diet from now on.

But our ancestors have always eaten meat, haven't they?

No! After much recent study and research, scientists have concluded that our early ancestors were vegetarians who ate no meat except during periods of extreme crisis. It was only during the last Ice Age, when their normal diet of fruits, nuts, and vegetables was unavailable, that the early humans had to start eating animal flesh in order to survive. Unfortunately the custom of eating meat continued after the Ice Age, either by necessity (like the Eskimos and tribes who live in the far north), or due to habit, conditioning, or lack of proper knowledge. However, throughout history there have been many individuals and groups of people who have realized the importance of a pure diet for health, mental clarity, or spiritual upliftment and have therefore remained vegetarians.

But isn't it natural for human beings to eat meat?

No! Scientists know that the diet of any animal corresponds to its physiological structure. Human physiology, bodily functions, and digestive system are completely different from those of carnivorous animals. According to diet we can divide vertebrate animals into three groups: meat eaters, grass-and-leaf eaters, and fruit eaters. Let us look closely at each and see where humanity fits in.

Meat eaters

Carnivorous animals, including the lion, dog, wolf, cat, etc., have many unique characteristics which set them apart from all other members of the animal kingdom. They all possess a very simple and short digestive system—only three times the length of their bodies. This is because flesh decays very rapidly, and the products of this decay quickly poison the bloodstream if they remain too long in the body. So a short digestive tract was evolved for rapid expulsion of putrefactive bacteria from decomposing flesh, as well as a stomach with ten times as much hydrochloric acid as a non-carnivorous animal (to digest fibrous tissue and bones). Meat eating animals that hunt in the cool of the night and sleep during the day when it is hot do not need sweat glands to cool their bodies, and therefore do not perspire through their skin, but rather sweat through their tongues. On the other hand, vegetarian animals, such as the cow, horse, zebra, deer, etc., spend much of their time in the sun gathering their food, and they freely perspire through their skin to cool their bodies. But the most significant difference between the natural meat eaters and other animals is their teeth. Along with sharp claws, all meat eaters, since they have to kill mainly with their teeth, possess powerful jaws and pointed, elongated, "canine" teeth to pierce tough hide and to spear and tear flesh. They do NOT have molars (flat, back teeth) which vegetarian animals need for grinding their food. Unlike grains, flesh does not need to be chewed in the mouth to predigest it; it is digested mostly in the stomach and the intestines. A cat, for example, can hardly chew at all.

Grass-and-leaf eaters

Grass-and-leaf-eating animals (elephant, cow, sheep, llama, etc.) live on grass, herbs, and other plants, much of which is coarse and bulky. The digestion of this type of food starts in the mouth with the enzyme ptyalin in the saliva. These foods must be chewed well and thoroughly mixed with ptyalin in order to be broken down. For this reason, grass-and-leaf eaters have 24 special "molar" teeth and a slight side-to-side motion to grind their food, as opposed to the exclusively up and down motion of carnivores. They have no claws or sharp teeth; they drink by sucking water up into their mouths as opposed to lapping it up with their tongue with all meat eaters do. Since they do not eat rapidly decaying foods like the meat eaters, and since their food can take a longer time to pass through their bodies, they have much longer digestive systems— intestines which are ten times the length of the body. Interestingly, recent studies have shown that a meat diet has an extremely harmful effect on these grass-and-leaf eaters. Dr. William Collins, a scientist in the New York Maimonides Medical Center, found that the meat-eating animals have an "almost unlimited capacity to handle saturated fats and cholesterol." But if a half pound of animal fat is added daily over a long period of time to a rabbit's diet, after two months its blood vessels become caked with fat and the serious disease called atherosclerosis develops. Human digestive systems, like the rabbit's, are also not designed to digest meat, and they become diseased the more it is eaten, as we will see later.

The fruit eaters

These animals include mainly the anthropoid apes, humanity's immediate animal ancestors. The diet of these apes consists mostly of fruits and nuts. Their skin has millions of pores for sweating, and they also have molars to grind and chew their food; their saliva is alkaline, and, like the grass and leaf eaters, it contains ptyalin for predigestion. Their intestines are extremely convoluted and are twelve times the length of their body, for the slow digestion of fruit and vegetables.

Human beings

Human characteristics are in every way like the fruit eaters, very similar to the grass eaters, and very unlike the meat eaters, as is clearly shown in the table on page 10. The human digestive system, tooth and jaw structure, and bodily functions are completely different from carnivorous animals. As in the case of the anthropoid ape, the human digestive system is twelve times the length of the body; our skin has millions of tiny pores to evaporate water and cool the body by sweating; we drink water by suction like all other vegetarian animals; our tooth and jaw structure is vegetarian; and our saliva is alkaline and contains ptyalin for predigestion of grains. Human beings clearly are not carnivores by physiology—our anatomy and digestive system show that we must have evolved for millions of years living on fruits, nuts, grains, and vegetables.

Furthermore, it is obvious that our natural instincts are noncarnivorous. Most people have other people kill their meat for them and would be sickened if they had to do the killing themselves. Instead of eating raw meat as all flesh-eating animals do, humans boil, bake, or fry it and disguise it with all kinds of sauces and spices so that it bears no resemblance to its raw state. One scientist explains it this way: "A cat will salivate with hungry desire at the smell of a piece of raw flesh but not at all at the smell of fruit. If people could delight in pouncing upon a bird, tear its still living limbs apart with their teeth, and suck the warm blood, one might conclude that nature provided them with meat-eating instinct. On the other hand, a bunch of lucious grapes makes their mouths water, and even in the absence of hunger they will eat fruit because it tastes so good." Scientists and naturalists, including the great evolutionist Charles Darwin, agree that early humans were fruit and vegetable eaters and that throughout history our anatomy has not changed. The Swedish scientist von Linne states, "The structure of human beings, external and internal, compared with that of the other animals, shows that fruit and succulent vegetables constitute their natural food."

So it is clear from scientific studies that physiologically, anatomically, and instinctively, human beings are perfectly suited to a diet of fruit, vegetables, nuts, and grains. This is summarized in the table on the following pages.

HISTORY OF VEGETARIANISM

From the beginnings of recorded history, we find that the vegetarian diet was regarded as the natural diet of humanity. The early Greeks, Egyptians, and Hebrews described human beings as fruit eaters. The wise priests of ancient Egypt never ate meat. Many great Greek sages—including Plato, Socrates, and Pythagoras—were strong advocates of the vegetarian diet. The great civilization of the Inca Indians was based on a vegetarian diet. In India the Buddha urged his disciples not to eat flesh. The Taoist saints and sages were vegetarians; and the early Christians and Jews were also. The Bible clearly states, "And God said, 'Behold, I have given you every herb-bearing seed, which is upon the face of the earth, and every tree, in which are fruits; for you it shall be as meat.'" (Genesis 1:29). And further, the Bible forbids the eating of flesh: "But living flesh and blood you shall not eat." (Genesis 9:4). St. Paul, one of the greatest disciples of Jesus, wrote in his letter to the Romans, "It is good not to eat flesh..." (Romans 14:21). Recently historians have discovered ancient texts similar to the New Testament describing the life and speeches of Jesus. In one of these scriptures Jesus says, "And the flesh of slain beasts in a person's body will become his own tomb. For I tell you truly, he who kills, kills himself, and whosoever eats the flesh of slain beasts eats the body of death." (*The Essene Gospel of Peace*).

The ancient Hindus in India always forbade the eating of meat. Manu, the first Hindu law-giver, wrote, "Meat can never be obtained without injury to living creatures, and if one injures conscious beings, one cannot attain heavenly bliss. Let all, therefore, shun meat." The holy book of Islam, the Koran, prohibits the eating of "dead animals, blood, and flesh..." One of the first and foremost disciples of Mohammed, his own nephew, advised the higher disciples, "Do not make your stomachs graves for animals."

MEAT EATER	LEAF-GRASS EATER
1. Has claws	No claws.
2. No pores on skin; perspires through tongue to cool body.	Perspires through millions of pores on skin.
3. Sharp, pointed front teeth to tear flesh.	No sharp, pointed front teeth.
4. Small salivary glands in the mouth (not needed to pre-digest grains and fruits).	Well-developed salivary glands, needed to pre-digest grains and fruits.
5. Acid saliva; no enzyme ptyalin to pre-digest grains.	Alkaline saliva; much ptyalin to pre-digest grains.
6. No flat back molar teeth to grind food.	Flat, back molar teeth to grind food.
7. Much strong hydrochloric acid in stomach to digest tough animal muscle, bone, etc.	Stomach acid 20 times less strong than meat-eaters.
8. Intestinal tract only 3 times body length so rapidly decaying meat can pass out of body quickly.	Intestinal tract 10 times body length; leaf and grains do not decay as quickly so they can pass more slowly through the body.

FRUIT EATER	HUMAN BEINGS
No claws.	No claws.
Perspires through millions of pores on skin.	Perspires through millions of pores on skin.
No sharp, pointed front teeth.	No sharp, pointed front teeth.
Well-developed salivary glands, needed to pre-digest grains and fruits.	Well-developed salivary glands, needed to pre-digest grains and fruits.
Alkaline saliva; much ptyalin to pre-digest grains.	Alkaline saliva; much ptyalin to pre-digest grains.
Flat, back molar teeth to grind food.	Flat, back molar teeth to grind food.
Stomach acid 20 times less strong than meat-eaters.	Stomach acid 20 times less strong than meat-eaters.
Intestinal tract 12 times body length; fruits do not decay as rapidly so they can pass more slowly through the body.	Intestinal tract 12 times body length.

So we see that throughout history, many wise and knowledgeable people have adopted the vegetarian diet and strongly urged others to do the same.

Some famous vegetarians

Plato, Socrates, Ovid, Seneca, Clement of Alexandria, Plutarch, Pythagoras, Leonardo da Vinci, Alexander Pope, Sir Isaac Newton, Jean Jacques Rousseau, Voltaire, John Milton, Charles Darwin, Percy Bysshe Shelley, Ralph Waldo Emerson, Henry David Thoreau, Richard Wagner, Benjamin Franklin, Leo Tolstoy, Louisa May Alcott, H. G. Wells, Mahatma Gandhi, Rabindranath Tagore, George Bernard Shaw, Albert Schweitzer, the Dalai Lama of Tibet, Albert Einstein.

WHAT ARE THE DANGERS OF MEAT EATING?

The Eskimos, living largely on meat and fat, age rapidly, with an average lifespan of 27 1/2 years. The Kirgese, a nomadic Eastern Russian tribe that live predominantly on meat, mature early and die equally early; they rarely pass the age of 40. In contrast, field investigations by anthropologists of non-meat cultures have documented the radiant health, stamina, and longevity enjoyed by people such as the Hunzas of Pakistan, the Otomi Tribe (natives of Mexico), and native peoples of the American Southwest. It is not uncommon for such tribes to have healthy and active individuals of 110 years or more. World health statistics consistently show that the nations which consume the most meat have the highest incidence of disease (heart disease, cancer), and groups of vegetarians in different countries have the lowest incidence of disease.*

Why do Meat Eaters Get More Diseases and Die Sooner?

Poisoning

Just before and during the agony of slaughter, the biochemistry of the terrified animal undergoes profound changes. Toxic byprod-

---

*In fact, a U.S. Senate nutrition commission in 1977 recommended as the "U.S. Dietary Goals" to "decrease consumption of meat and increase consumption of fruits, vegetables and whole grains."

ucts are forced throughout the body, thus pain-poisoning the entire carcass.

It is now a well-known fact that emotions produce great biochemical changes in the body, especially hormonal changes in the blood. Just as our bodies become ill during times of intense rage or fear, animals, no less than humans, undergo profound biochemical changes in dangerous situations. The hormone level in the animals' blood—especially the hormone adrenalin—changes radically as they see other animals dying around them and they struggle futilely for life and freedom. These large amounts of hormones remain in the meat and later poison the human tissue, and disturb the mind as well. According to the Nutrition Institute of America, "The flesh of an animal carcass is loaded with toxic blood and other waste byproducts."

Cancer

A study conducted among 50,000 vegetarians (the Seventh Day Adventists) revealed results that shook the world of cancer research. The study clearly showed that this group has an astonishingly low rate of cancer. All types of cancer occurred at significantly lower rates as compared with a group matched on age and sex. The study showed that the life expectancy of the Adventists is also significantly longer. A recent study of Mormons in California showed that cancer occurs in this group at a rate of 50% less than in the normal population. Mormons characteristically eat little meat.

Why do meat eaters get more cancer? One reason might be the fact that animal flesh which is several days old naturally turns a sickly grey-green color. The meat industry tries to mask this discoloration by adding nitrites, nitrates, and other preservatives. These substances make the meat appear red, but in recent years many of them have repeatedly been shown to be carcinogenic (cancer-inducing).

Said Dr. William Lijinsky, a cancer researcher at Oak Ridge National Laboratory in Tennessee, "I don't even feed nitrate-laden foods to my cat."

Moreover, British and American scientists who have studied intestinal bacteria of meat eaters as compared to vegetarians have found significant differences. The bacteria in the meat eaters' intestines react with the digestive juices to produce chemicals which have been found to cause cancer. This may explain why cancer of the bowel is very prevalent in meat-eating areas like North American and Western Europe, while it is extremely rare in vegetarian countries such as India. In the United States, for example, bowel cancer is the second most common form of cancer (second only to lung cancer), and the people of Scotland, who eat 20% more beef than the English, have one of the world's highest rates of cancer of the bowel.

Chemical diet

Eating meat has often been called "eating on top of the food chain." In nature there is a long chain of eaters: plants "eat" sunlight, air, and water; animals eat plants; larger animals or human beings eat smaller animals. Now, all over the world fields are being treated with poisonous chemical fertilizers and pesticides. These poisons are retained in the bodies of the animals that eat the plants and grasses. For instance, fields are sprayed with the insect-killing chemical DDT, a very powerful poison which scientists say can cause cancer, sterility, and serious liver disease. DDT and pesticides like it are retained in animal (and fish) fat and, once stored, are difficult to break down. Thus, as cows eat grass or feed, whatever pesticides they eat are mostly retained, so that when you eat meat, you are taking into your body all the concentrations of DDT and other chemicals that have accumulated during the animal's lifetime. Eating at the "top" of the food chain, humans become the final consumer and thus the recipient of the highest concentration of poisonous pesticides. In fact, meat contains 13 times as much DDT as vegetables, fruits, and grass. This is especially harmful to newborn babies, whose tiny bodies receive all the concentrated poisons from their meat-eating mothers. Experiments performed at Iowa State University showed that most of the DDT in human bodies comes from meat, and the average concentration of DDT in the bodies of vegetarians was less than half that of meat-eaters!

But the poisoning of the meat does not stop here. Meat animals are treated with many more chemicals to increase their growth, fatten them quickly, improve their meat color, etc. In order to produce the most meat at the highest profit, animals are force-fed, injected with hormones to stimulate growth, given appetite-stimulants, antibiotics, sedatives, and chemical feed mixtures. The *New York Times* reported, "But of far greater potential danger to the consumer's health are the hidden contaminants—bacteria-like salmonella and residues from the use of pesticides, nitrates, nitrites, hormones, antibiotics, and other chemicals." (July 18, 1971). Many of these have been found to be cancer-causing chemicals, and, in fact, many animals die of these drugs even before they are led to slaughter. Studies have shown that many of these chemicals in meat and fish can cause cancer and many other diseases, deform an unborn baby, and cause great harm to pregnant women and small children. Thus pregnant mothers should be especially careful of their diet to insure the mental and physical health of their newborn child.

Animals' diseases

Another danger facing meat eaters is that animals are frequently infected with diseases which are undetected or simply ignored by the meat producers or inspectors.

As farms have evolved into animal factories, many animals never see the light of day—their lives are spent in cramped and cruel surroundings which culminate in a brutal death. A case in point is the high-rise chicken farms. According to an article in the *Chicago Tribune*, eggs are hatched on the top floor, where the chicks are stimulated, drugged, and force-fed. They eat ravenously in their tiny cages, never getting exercise or fresh air. As they grow they are moved, one floor at a time, to lower levels. When they arrive at the bottom floor they are slaughtered. Such unnatural practices not only imbalance the body chemistry of the chickens and destroy their natural habits, but, unfortunately, often stimulate the growth of malignant tumors and other malformations.

Often, if an animal has cancer or a tumor in a certain part of its body, the cancerous part will be cut away and the rest of the body, full of toxins and disease, will be sold as meat. Or worse yet, the tumors themselves will be incorporated into mixed meats such as hot dogs, and euphemistically labeled "parts." In one area of America, where there is routine inspection of slaughtered animals, 25,000 cattle with eye cancers were sold as beef! Scientists have found experimentally that if the liver of a diseased animal is fed to fish, the fish will get cancer. A famous vegetarian doctor, Dr. J. H.

Kellogg, once remarked when he sat down to a vegetarian dinner, "It's nice to eat a meal and not have to worry about what your food may have died of."

No one knows better than the meat inspectors themselves how much disease there is among the animals slaughtered for food. Once a lady attending a dinner ordered a vegetable plate instead of the regular meal. Beside her sat a gentleman she had not met before. She and the gentleman looked at each others' vegetable dinners until finally he asked her, "Excuse me, are you a vegetarian?"

"Yes, I am," she answered. "Are you?"

"No," he replied. "I'm a meat inspector."

Heart disease

Perhaps the single most compelling argument for a non-meat diet, however, is the undeniable and well-documented correlation between meat eating and heart disease. Heart disease is very common in societies where much meat is consumed, such as the USA, Canada, western Europe and Australia, but practically unheard of in societies where meat consumption is low.

What is it that makes meat so harmful to the circulatory system? The fats of animal flesh, such as cholesterol, do not break down well in the human body, and instead begin to line the walls of the meat eater's blood vessels. With the process of continual accumulation, the opening inside the vessels gets smaller and smaller as the years go by, allowing less and less blood to flow through. This dangerous condition is called atherosclerosis; it places a tremendous burden on the heart which has to pump harder and harder to send the blood through clogged and constricted vessels. As a result, high blood pressure, strokes, and heart attacks occur.*

Scientists at Harvard found that the average blood pressure of vegetarians studied was significantly lower than that of a comparable group of non-vegetarians. During the Korean War, 200 bodies of young American soldiers, averaging about 22 years old, were examined after death. Almost 80% had hardened

---

*Fried foods are also more likely to cause this dangerous condition of atherosclerosis, especially when starches are fried in fats. Thus heart doctors advise their patients to avoid fried foods, cakes and pastries, potato chips, etc.

arteries, clogged with waste from eating meat. Korean soldiers of the same age group were examined and were found to be free of this damage to their blood vessels. The Koreans were basically vegetarians. In America heart disease is the number one killer: one out of two people die of heart or related blood vessel disease. More and more physicians (and the American Heart Association) are sharply restricting the amount of meat that their heart patients can eat, or are telling them to stop eating it entirely. The *Journal of the American Medical Association* reported in 1961 that "a vegetarian diet can prevent 90-97% of heart diseases (thrombo-embolic disease and coronary occlusions)."

Scientists now recognize that the roughage and fiber of vegetarian diets actually lower the level of cholesterol. Dr. U. D. Register, Chairman of the Department of Nutrition at Loma Linda University in California, describes experiments in which a diet rich in beans, peas, etc., actually reduced cholesterol, even while the subjects were eating large amounts of butter.

Putrefaction

As soon as an animal is killed, proteins in its body coagulate, and self-destruct enzymes are released (unlike slow decaying plants which have a rigid cell wall and simple circulatory system. Soon, denatured substances, called ptomaines, are formed. Due to these ptomaines that are released immediately after death, animal flesh, fish, and eggs have a common property—extremely rapid decomposition and putrefaction. By the time the animal is slaughtered, placed in cold storage, "aged," transported to the butcher's shop, purchased, brought home, stored, prepared, and eaten, one can imagine what stage of decay one's dinner is in.

Meat passes very slowly through the human digestive system, which, as we have seen, is not designed to digest it. It takes meat about five days to pass out of the body (as opposed to vegetarian food, which takes only 1 1/2 days); during this time the disease-causing products of decaying meat are in constant contact with the digestive organs. The habit of eating animal flesh in its characteristic state of decomposition creates a poisonous state in the colon and wears out the intestinal tract prematurely.

Raw meat, being always in a state of decay, can contaminate

cooks' hands and everything it comes into contact with. British public health officers, after an outbreak of food poisoning originating in slaughter houses, warned housewives to "handle raw meat as if it were hygienically equivalent to cow dung." Often poisonous bacteria are not destroyed even by cooking, especially if the meat is undercooked, barbecued, or roasted on a spit; these are notorious sources of infection.

Kidney disease, gout, arthritis

Among the most prominent wastes that a meat eater loads his body with are urea and uric acid (nitrogen compounds). Beefsteak, for example, contains about 14 grams of uric acid per pound. Research has shown that the kidneys of meat-eaters have to do three times the amount of work to eliminate poisonous nitrogen compounds in meat than do the kidneys of vegetarians. When people are young, they are usually able to bear this extra burden so that no evidence of injury or disease appears; but, as the kidneys age and become worn out prematurely, they become unable to do their work efficiently, and kidney disease is the frequent result.

When kidneys can no longer handle the excessively heavy load of a meat-eating diet, the unexcreted uric acid is deposited throughout the body. There it is absorbed by the muscles like a sponge, soaking up water, and later it can harden and form crystals. When this happens in the joints, the painful conditions of gout, arthritis, and rheumatism result; when the uric acid collects in the nerves, neuritis and sciatica result. Now many doctors are advising patients suffering from these diseases to stop eating meat completely or to drastically reduce the amount they eat.

Thus all these accumulated toxins make meat a highly impure food. The *Encyclopedia Brittanica* states, "Toxic wastes, including uric acid, are present in the blood and tissue of meat animals, as well as virulent bacteria, not only from the putrefactory process but also from animal diseases. Furthermore, meat contains vaccines injected in the animals... On the other hand, proteins obtained from nuts, beans, grains and dairy products are relatively pure as compared to meat which has a 56% impure water content."

Poor elimination

Since our digestive system was not designed for a meat diet, poor elimination is a natural consequence and distressingly common complaint of meat eaters. Meat, being extremely low in fiber, has this major disadvantage—it moves very sluggishly through the human digestive tract (four times slower than grain and vegetable foods) making chronic constipation a common ailment in meat-eating societies. (It takes food half as long to pass through the intestines of an African, who eats much fiber in his or her diet, as through the intestines of an American, who eats little.)

Much recent research has shown conclusively that a healthy elimination pattern requires the bulk and fiber available only from a proper vegetarian diet. Vegetables, whole grains and fruits, in contrast to meat, retain moisture and bind bulk for easy passage. Vegetarians get generous portions of natural food fiber in their diet and benefit tremendously from the disease-preventive characteristics of this substance. According to present research, natural fiber may be a significant deterrent of appendicitis, diverticulitis, cancer of the colon, heart disease, and obesity.

VEGETARIANS ARE FAR HEALTHIER THAN MEAT EATERS

As we have seen, meat is not the natural or the most healthy diet for human beings. We can survive on it, of course, but it prematurely wears out the human body and creates many diseases. "A gasoline engine can operate on kerosene, but it will clog frequently, wear out sooner, and break down faster than if it were run on gasoline." And our bodies are not just machines, but intricate and beautiful creations which are to serve us our entire lifetime. It therefore stands to reason that they should be given the food which they were built to consume—a natural diet of fruit, grains, nuts, legumes, vegetables, and dairy products.

It is no wonder, then, that countless studies have proved that vegetarians all over the world are far healthier than those who eat meat.

During the economic crisis of war, when people were forced to live on vegetarian diets, their health dramatically improved. In Denmark during World War I, there was a danger of an acute food shortage due to the British blockade. The Danish government appointed the director of the national vegetarian society to direct the rationing program. For the duration of the blockade the Danes were forced to subsist on grains, vegetables, fruits, and dairy products. In the first year of the rationing, the death rate fell 17%. When the people of Norway became vegetarians due to the food shortage of World War I, there was an immediate drop in the death rate from circulatory diseases. When the people of both Norway and Denmark returned to a meat diet after the war, their death rate and heart disease rate promptly rose to pre-war levels.

The Hunzas, a tribe in north India and Pakistan, have become internationally known for their freedom from disease and long life. Curious scientists from many lands have flocked to their villages to discover the secret of a culture where disease is almost unknown and natives often reach ages of 115 or more. Their diet consists mainly of whole grains, fresh fruits, vegetables, and goat's milk. Wrote Sir Rob McGarrison, a British general and doctor who worked with the Hunzas, "I never saw a case of appendicitis, colitis, or cancer."

Recently, a group of Harvard doctors and research scientists went to a remote village of 400 people in the mountains of Ecuador. They were amazed to find that many of the native people lived to extraordinarily old ages. One man was 121 years old, and several were over 100. A thorough examination was given to those over the age of 75. Of these only two showed any evidence of heart disease! The villagers were pure vegetarians. The doctors called these findings "extraordinary" and said that "such examination of a similar population in the United States would show 95% with heart disease."

Statistically, vegetarians are thinner and healthier. On the average, vegetarians weigh about 20 pounds less than meat eaters. The American National Institute of Health, in a recent study of 50,000 vegetarians, found that the vegetarians live longer, have significantly lower incidence of heart disease, and have an impressively lower rate of cancer as compared to meat-eating Americans.

In England vegetarians have to pay much less for life insurance than meat eaters because they are less likely to get heart disease and so are considered less of a risk by the insurance companies. And vegetarian restaurants pay less for their food poisoning insurance policies since their customers are much less likely to be poisoned by the food than in restaurants which serve meat.

At Harvard University a doctor has shown that a vegetarian diet reduces colds and allergies.

Studies of children have shown that vegetarian children have better teeth and much less incidence of childrens' diseases—colds, allergies, etc.—than non-vegetarian children, and are less prone to obesity and heart disease.

So it has been scientifically proven again and again that meat eating is positively harmful to the human body, while a well-selected vegetarian diet in harmony with the law of nature will help us have a dynamically healthy body, a pure temple for the elevated thoughts and feelings of the mind.

VEGETARIANS ARE MORE PHYSICALLY FIT THAN MEAT EATERS

One of the greatest misconceptions about the vegetarian diet is that it will produce a weak, pale, sickly person. Nothing could be farther from the truth. Many studies, in fact, have shown vegetarians to be stronger, more agile, and to have more endurance than meat eaters.

Dr. H. Schouteden at the University of Belgium conducted tests to compare endurance, strength, and quickness of recovery from fatigue in vegetarians and meat eaters. His findings indicated that vegetarians were substantially superior in all three characteristics.

In endurance tests conducted at Yale University by Dr. Irving Fisher, on Yale athletes, instructors, doctors and nurses, it was found that vegetarians had over twice the stamina of meat eaters. Similar tests by J. H. Kellogg at Battle Creek Sanitarium in Michigan confirmed Fisher's findings.

A study at Brussels University by Dr. J. Ioteyko and V. Kipani found that vegetarians were able to perform endurance tests two to three times longer than the meat eaters before complete exhaustion, and they took only one-fifth the time to recover from fatigue after each test than their meat-eating counterparts.

These striking results show that the vegetarian diet is superior for physical strength, endurance, and efficiency. Indeed, the world's most powerful and longest lived animals are all vegetarians. The horse, oxen, buffalo, and elephant all have the healthy bodies, the power of endurance, and the phenomenal strength that enables them to carry massive loads and do arduous work for man. None of the flesh-eating animals have the stamina or endurance to be beasts of burden. It is also interesting to note how many great athletes who have set world records have been vegetarians.

The Vegetarian Cycling Club in England has held over 40% of the national cycling records, and all over Europe the vegetarian cyclists have consistently made up a higher percentage of winners than the meat-eating cyclists.

The great vegetarian swimmer, Murray Rose, was the youngest triple gold medal winner in the Olympic games. He has been hailed as one of the greatest swimmers of all time and has broken many records. A British vegetarian swam across the English channel faster than anyone in history—in 6 hours and 20 minutes.

Many internationally famous athletes, past and present, changed to a vegetarian diet and found their performance improved: for example, the Austrian weight lifter, A. Anderson, who won many world records, and Johnny Weismuller, who made 56 world swimming records. They report no decrease in strength; in fact, their ability seems to increase.

Bill Walton, the well-known American basketball star center, is famous for his aggressive, hard-driving performance. His personal experience has so convinced him of the benefits of a vegetarian diet that he has repeatedly advocated this regimen for others.

All over the world, vegetarians have set many records—in wrestling, boxing, walking, football, cross-country running, etc. Vegetarians actually have more endurance and energy because their bodies do not have to waste tremendous amounts of energy trying to counteract the poisons in meat.

BUT WILL I GET ENOUGH NUTRITION WITHOUT EATING MEAT?

Proteins—the building blocks of life
One of the worries people have when they think about adopting a vegetarian diet is, "Will I get enough nutrition if I don't eat meat? Will I get enough protein?" They have nothing to worry about: a

vegetarian diet can provide all necessary body nutrients. In fact, many studies have shown that a vegetarian diet provides much more nutritional energy than a meat diet.

Of all the nutrients needed by our bodies, one of the most important is protein. Since most of our body tissues are formed of protein, it is necessary for growth and repair; it is also n important component in the hormones and enzyme systems in our body which direct and regulate many of the body's processes; and it is essential to build antibodies in the blood, to fight infection and disease.

Too much protein is harmful to health

Many people think that we need to eat a great deal of protein during the day, especially if we are active. We have been conditioned—often by massive advertising campaigns—to believe that meat eating is essential for health. This is a great misconception. In fact, we need far less protein than we think we do, and recent medical research has proven that eating too much protein harms the liver and kidneys and is the cause of many diseases. Millions of people in the wealthy industrialized nations who are consuming tremendous quantities of meat are actually eating 2 or 3 times the amount of protein they need. The excess is converted into carbohydrates and stored as fat. Thus over 50% of Americans are overweight* and prone to many diseases directly related to obesity, especially high blood pressure and heart disease.

"Good" and "bad" proteins?

Another great misconception is that vegetable protein is inferior to meat protein. In the 1950's scientists classified meat protein as "first class" and vegetable protein as "second class." However, this idea has since been completely disproved, because vegetable proteins have been found to be equally as effective and nutritious as meat proteins; now this distinction has been discarded.**

In fact, some vegetarian foods, such as the incredibly protein-rich soybean, has twice the amount of protein found in meat!

---

*Whereas vegetarians, as we have seen, weigh about 20 pounds less than meat eaters.
**The authoritative British medical journal, *The Lancet*, stated, "From a nutritional point of view, animal and vegetable proteins should not be differentiated."

(Soybeans are 40% protein, whereas even the leanest cut of beef steak has only 20% usable protein). Many nuts, seeds and beans contain 30% protein:

FOOD (100 gms.)	GRAMS OF PROTEIN
Soy Milk (powdered)	41.8
Soybeans (dry)	31.4
Milk (powdered)	26.4
Peanuts	26.0
Beans	24.7
Beef	20.2
Chicken	18.6
Lamb	16.8

"Essential" amino acids & "complete proteins"

Proteins are constituted from smaller molecules called amino acids. When protein is ingested, it is broken down into its constituent amino acids which are then utilized individually or reassembled into the various types of protein the body needs. There are about 22 amino acids, of which all but 8 "essential" amino acids can normally be synthesized in the body. If any one of these 8 amino acids is missing, the others cannot be utilized; thus all of the 8 amino acids have to be present at the same meal. These 8 essential amino acids must also be present in certain proportions; if the proper proportion of even one is lacking, the remaining amino acids are correspondingly reduced, and consequently the body receives less available protein for its use. Foods or food combinations providing all the essential amino acids in the requisite proportion are said to contain a complete protein.

Meat is not the only complete protein, and in fact many meats lack one or more of the essential amino acids. Soybeans and milk are also complete proteins; and combining several foods makes a high quality food that far surpasses the protein value of either food alone.

The following food combinations have been found by nutrition experts to produce complete proteins:

MILK with rice, wheat, peanuts, sesame, beans, or potatoes
BEANS with rice, wheat, corn, nuts, or sesame seeds
PEANUTS with rice, wheat, corn or oats
SOYBEANS with wheat, corn or sesame
VEGETABLES with rice or any other grain, or sesame

Rural people everywhere in the world seem to complement their proteins instinctively, for instance by mixing rice and tofu or beans (as in China or India), or corn and beans (as in Central and South America).

In 1972 Dr. Frederick Stare of Harvard University conducted a comprehensive study of vegetarians (including adult men and women, pregnant women, and adolescent girls and boys). He found that all groups were consuming over twice their minimum daily protein requirement. In 1954 scientists conducted a detailed study at Harvard and found that when a variety of vegetable, grain, and dairy products were eaten in ANY combination, there was always more than enough protein; they were unable to find a protein deficiency no matter what combinations were used. The scientists concluded that it is very difficult to eat a varied vegetarian diet which will not easily meet all protein requirements for the human body.

In newspapers we often read about the malnourished people in poor countries who are starving and dying from protein deficiency, and we often blame this on their vegetarian diet. But scientists have found that these people are undernourished not because they are not eating meat, but because they are not eating enough food. A diet of rice only (and very little of that) or sweet potatoes only, naturally leads to malnutrition and early death. By contrast, anywhere in this world that one can find people living on a vegetarian diet with an adequate caloric intake and an adequate variety of vegetables, grains and legumes, there one will find strong, healthy, and thriving people.

Soybeans—the miracle bean
More than a billion people every day eat a source of protein

which is only now beginning to be discovered in the West—tofu, made from soybeans, one of the most nutritious and inexpensive foods in the world.

For thousands of years the people of the Orient have eaten soybeans, and this may indeed be one of the secrets of their longevity, endurance and youthful vitality. Soybeans have been variously called "the magic plant," "yellow diamonds," "the miracle bean," "gold from the earth," and "the meat that grows on vines," because of their high protein content and richness in vitamins and minerals.

Soybeans contain twice as much protein as the same weight of meat, with all the 8 essential amino acids in the proper proportions. Many meat proteins are deficient in one or more of the essential amino acids, thus making much of the meat protein unutilizable. Soy protein is thus better assimilated in the digestive tract, and, in contrast to meat, contains no hard fats, no fattening starch or high calories, no cholesterol-forming* ingredients, no uric acid formations, no chemicals or infectious animal diseases. Moreover, soybeans contain more vitamin B than any other plant food— much more than the daily requirement, and are rich in Vitamins A and D.

Recently researchers have tapped the secret of the soybean and discovered its youth-building, magic ingredient—lecithin. Lecithin plays a decisive role in stimulating metabolism throughout all the cells of the body: it increases memory and strengthens the glands and regenerates body tissues; it improves blood circulation and respiration; and it strengthens the bones and increases resistance to injury. In cases of nervous exhaustion or lack of energy, lecithin in soybeans will restore lost energy and strength.

Now more and more westerners are realizing what Orientals have known for centuries—that lecithin-rich soybeans promote strength and endurance, agility and flexibility, youthfulness and vitality. And they are far more economical as well: because of rising meat prices, housewives, companies, and even governments are beginning to serve their families and employees soybeans instead of meat.

---

* Soybeans contain no cholesterol and in fact have been shown in tests to actually reduce the cholesterol level in the blood.

Carbohydrates: the body's fuel

If proteins are the building blocks of the body, carbohydrates are the body's fuel, providing us with the heat and energy we need to function every day. For vegetarians the principal sources of carbohydrates are grains and beans, sugars and fruits, potatoes, etc.

It is now generally recognized that we need much less carbohydrates than we eat, and one of the principal health problems in many countries is that people eat too many "empty calories" (carbohydrates which provide many calories but few vitamins, minerals and proteins)—too much rice or bread, and too many sweets. As one nutrition expert stated, "Physiologically it is best to eat carbohydrates that furnish body-building elements—vitamins, minerals and protein—as well as calories. This means whole grain cereals and breads, barley, rye, and brown rice in preference to white. It also means minimizing the use of white sugar and its products—candy, sugary drinks, jelly and jam, and other similar stomach-filling but body-starving concoctions."

An increasing number of people all over the world are turning to less refined and processed foods, realizing that not only are they more nutritious, but also high in fiber which is essential for proper digestion.

FOOD(100g.)	Protein(g)	Calcium	Phos	Iron	Potas	Sod	VitB1	VitB2
Brown rice	7.5	32	221	1.6	214	9	.34	.05
White rice	6.7	24	94	.8	92	5	.07	.03
WWflour	13.3	51	342	3.3	370	3	.55	.12
White flour	10.5	16	87	.08	95	2	.06	.05
Molasses		85	19	3.4	344	30	.01	.03
Honey		5	6	.5	51	5	tr	.04
White sugar		0	0	.1	3	1	0	0

Sugar: "white poison"

There are a number of different kinds of sugars:

GLUCOSE

Glucose is the primary energy source of the body; the brain especially relies on it. It is manufactured from the carbohydrates we eat—the simple sugars (found naturally in fruit, vegetables, and dairy products), and starches (in grains, legumes and vegetables).

28

With no sucrose (white sugar) added to the diet, the body is able to produce adequate glucose.

SUCROSE

Sucrose is the most common form of refined sugar—white or "table sugar."* Refined white sugar not only provides empty calories but it lacks the very vitamins and minerals which are needed for its own metabolism, and thus it robs the body of the nutrients obtained from other foods.

There are many health problems related to the consumption of refined sugar. First of all, sugar makes the teeth sticky, so that foods and bacteria in the mouth adhere to the teeth; the acids produced by the bacteria then eat away at the teeth, resulting in dental cavities.

But there are more severe metabolic stresses. Sugars consumed in their natural state (like fruits and grains) are broken down and released into the bloodstream slowly, so the body can easily assimilate them. But refined sugars raise the blood sugar rapidly; this "rush" is followed by an equally rapid "crash" which often leaves one feeling tired, irritable or depressed. Frequently, as energy falls, one's response is to reach for more sugar, since it will quickly relieve the "down" feeling. What is really needed at this time is a high-protein food which will gradually pick up the energy level and supply other important nutrients as well.

The blood sugar roller-coaster can lead to emotional instability and confusion, dizziness, and headache. In addition, over-consumption of sugar can trigger a craving similar to the physiological dependence produced by drugs. People who try to stop eating sugar generally find it a great struggle; it may feel like a real addiction.

These symptoms, along with drowsiness, forgetfulness, or a general "spaced-out feeling" are typical symptoms of hypoglycemia (low blood sugar). During the body's chemical chain reaction in hypoglycemia triggered by eating an excess of refined sugar, adrenalin is released by the adrenal glands, creating a stress throughout

---

*Brown sugar is merely sucrose with caramel coloring or a bit of molasses mixed in. Honey and maple syrup both contain small amounts of vitamins and minerals, so they are less of a metabolic drain.

the body and mind. For this reason many Oriental nutritionists call refined sugar a "white poison."

Sugar also depresses the activity of the white blood cells, lowering resistance to infection, and it may also lead to the development of diabetes.

Those who want to avoid sugar should substitute honey, maple syrup, or barley malt; and for snacks, eat fruits and juices instead of sugary sweets. Cutting down on sugar may produce immediate withdrawal symptoms such as depression, fatigue or irritability; but these should ease within about a week; and as the taste buds become more sensitive, the natural sweetness of ripe fruits, vegetables and grains will be savored more and more. Life without refined sugar can be just as sweet!

Fats

Fats store energy in various parts of the body for use over a long period of time, and they also protect the body from cold and injury. The vegetarians' principal source of fats are vegetable oils (soybeans, sesame, peanut, corn, etc.) milk, butter and cheese, peanuts and other nuts, sesame and other seeds. These natural vegetable oils contain certain essential fats which cannot be obtained by eating meat, and they do not produce the harmful cholesterol in the body which, as we have seen, lines the blood vessels and causes serious heart and blood vessel disease.

Minerals

Minerals perform many important functions in the body; they are essential elements for almost all the chemical reactions and are necessary for the formation of bones, muscles, nerves, and blood. They are also essential for the transmission of nervous impulses and for digestion. Without sufficient amounts of all the different essential minerals, many diseases will result. Some of the most important minerals needed by our bodies, and where to obtain them, are described following.

Iron

Iron is a very essential mineral which helps carry oxygen in the blood to the cells. A deficiency in iron results in anemia, with persistent symptoms of fatigue, headaches, weakness, breathlessness, dizziness, forgetfulness, and mental dullness*. A simple blood test can be taken to check for iron deficiency. Iron can easily be obtained in a vegetarian diet by eating plenty of green vegetables, soybeans, dried fruits, beans, or whole meal bread. Wheat germ, the most nutritious part of the wheat grain, is also an excellent source of iron; it is usually refined out of the grain when it is milled into white flour, but it can be bought separately and roasted or eaten raw, sprinkled on other foods or cereals.

Iron is water soluble, so it may be lost if the water vegetables are cooked in is thrown out. In fact, cooking in cast-iron pots will increase the iron content in foods. Iron deficiency anemia is a common problem among young children, adolescents and women; menstruation causes the loss of iron, which is why women have a higher need for iron than adult men, and a much higher incidence of anemia. Women, especially pregnant women, and growing children should be very careful to obtain enough iron; an easy way is to substitute molasses (high in iron) for sugar. (Iron absorption is greatly aided by vitamin C foods).

Recommended sources of iron (per 100 gm):
Yeast 17.3 mg.
Wheat germ 9.4 mg.
Dried fruits (apricots, raisins, prunes) 5.5 mg.
Beans & soybeans 3 mg.
Spinach & beet greens 3 mg.

Calcium
Calcium is needed to build bones and teeth, and to help the blood to clot. It is also a catalyst in many biological reactions, and is necessary in the transmission of nervous impulses throughout the body. Calcium deficiency may cause frequent backaches, tense nerves, restlessness, irritability, and insomnia. The best source of calcium is milk: a natural "cure" for insomnia is to drink a warm glass of milk at night before going to bed. Other excellent sources of calcium are (per 100 gm):

---

*Longitudinal ridges in the fingernails are a tell-tale sign of anemia, as well as facial pallor.

Calcium content (per 100 gm):
Turnip greens 246 mg.
Almonds 234 mg.
Kale 179 mg.
Milk 118 mg.
Sesame butter 110 mg.
Spinach 93 mg.
Broccoli 88 mg.
Soybeans 73 mg.
Dried apricots 67 mg.

Iodine

Iodine is essential for the functioning of one of the most important glands of the body the thyroid gland, which regulates the metabolism and growth of the entire body. A lack of iodine results in fatigue, low blood pressure, and a tendency to gain weight easily. In severe cases this can cause goiter, the enlargement of the thyroid gland. Seaweed is especially rich in iodine; other good sources are spinach, turnips, milk, radishes, unrefined salt and iodized refined salt.

Sodium & potassium

Sodium and potassium are essential to maintain the pH and fluid balance in the body. They are both involved in muscle relaxation and a potassium deficiency may cause muscle tension. An excess of sodium (from salt) will reduce the amount of potassium in the body, so potassium deficiency is usually related to excessive salt intake. Thus consuming a large amount of salt may directly contribute to muscular tension. (However, pregnant women apparently have a greater need for sodium than other people). Potassium is highly water soluble, so care should be taken to use all cooking water.

Phosphorus

Phosphorus is necessary for energy metabolism, and is found in milk products, brewer's yeast, wheat bran and germ, rice bran, legumes, nuts and seeds.

Magnesium

Magnesium is needed in proportion to the amount of calcium needed. Magnesium deficiency is thought to increase one's susceptibility to cardio-vascular disease. Good sources of magnesium are nuts, soybeans, whole grains, and leafy vegetables.

Vitamins

Vitamins are not foods, but catalysts which direct the chemical reactions in our body's metabolism. They are present in very small amounts in most foods, and if they are lacking from the diet, a large variety of diseases may result. The most important vitamins are discussed below:

VITAMIN A

Vitamin A is important for the eyes; a slight deficiency impairs the vision. A common symptom of vitamin A deficiency is night blindness and frequent eyestrain. Those who work in very bright or dim light, or who read or sew a great deal, need plenty of vitamin A in their food, otherwise impairment of the vision will result. Vitamin A is also necessary for healthy skin and hair; a deficiency may cause pimples, dandruff, dry or rough skin, dry and dull hair, and peeling nails. Vitamin A also helps maintain the health of the mucous membranes in the respiratory tract and other parts of the body, and a lack may result in infections in these areas. The best source of vitamin A is raw carrots, but it is also found in leafy green vegetables, sweet potatoes, broccoli, squash, apricots and milk. Even one serving of any of these vegetables will supply the daily vitamin A requirements.

Vitamin A content in Units:

Carrots (raw) 11,000
Spinach 8,100
Sweet potatoes 8,100
Fresh apricots 8,000
Kale 7,400
Beet greens 5,100
Squash 4,200
Butter 3,300
Broccoli 2,000
Milk 140

The B vitamins

The B vitamins are closely related compounds often found together in foods, that are involved in dozens of body functions, including growth, energy metabolism, the maintenance of the nervous system, proper kidney functioning, etc. Every cell of the body needs the B vitamins, and if these are deficient, the whole body suffers; this may result in stunted growth in young children. The most common symptoms of deficiency include irritability, inefficiency, depression, mental sluggishness, fatigue, confusion, worry, instability, moodiness, bad breath, and canker sores in the mouth.*

The best vegetarian sources of the B-complex are leafy green vegetables, whole grains, nutritional yeast, wheat germ, rice polish, and sprouts. Meat eaters eat sparingly, if at all, of most of these foods, and this combined with the prevalence of refined and processed foods, unfortunately has made vitamin B deficiency increasingly common.

Nutritional yeast contains a balance of B vitamins close to the proportions found in the human body, and may be taken as a natural B vitamin supplement when needed to restore health. Many people find that mixing a tablespoon or two of yeast into orange juice or milk is the easiest way to take the yeast.

All the B vitamins are water soluble, so the cooking water of vegetables should always be eaten, never thrown out.

VITAMIN B3 (NIACIN)

Do you often feel sad and irritable? It may be because you lack Vitamin B3, often called the "morale-boosting vitamin." Niacin plays an important role in the release of energy from the food we eat, and so if it is lacking, our bodies do not receive enough energy to function properly, no matter how much food we eat. Volunteers in scientific experiments who deliberately ate a diet lacking in Vitamin B3, soon became fearful, anxious and mentally confused. They found themselves becoming daily more and more tense, moody, forgetful and depressed. However, these unpleasant symp-

---

*A sure indication of vitamin B deficiency is the tongue: the taste buds at the top and sides will become smooth, and gradually grooves will form on the tongue, especially down the center.

toms were eliminated in a few hours with sufficient doses of vitamin B3. (Some vitamin B3 deficiencies also result in digestive trouble and pellagra.) Thus many physicians are now successfully treating mental patients with massive doses of vitamin B3. The best natural sources of B3 are (per 100 gm):*

Vitamin B3 content (per 100 gm):
Yeast 38 mg.
Wheat bran 21 mg.
Peanuts 17.2
Almonds & beans 3

VITAMIN B2 (RIBOFLAVIN)

Vitamin B2 is necessary to help the body produce and use the proteins it needs. A deficiency in vitamin B2 results in soreness and inflammation of the mouth and lips, dry and scaly skin, watery and burning eyes, eye strain and sensitivity to light. Some of the best sources of vitamin B2 are (per 100 gm):

Vitamin B2 content (per 100 gm):
Yeast 4.28 mg.
Almonds .92 mg
Wheat germ .68 gm.
Milk .17 mg.
Whole wheat bread .15 mg.
Spinach .14 mg.
Peanuts .13 mg.

VITAMIN B1 (THIAMINE)

Like vitamin B3, vitamin B1 is also necessary to help the body produce energy from the food we eat, and lack of it will also result in fatigue and exhaustion. Vitamin B1 also adjusts the blood pressure, activates the nerves, and helps maintain the body's metabolic rate. A deficiency produces poisonous acids which harm the brain and nerve cells. Volunteers who ate a diet lacking in vitamin B1

---

*Some doctors contend that hose with symptoms of vitamin B3 deficiency are actually getting enough in their diet, but are unable to utilize it due to weakness in the adrenal glands. Yoga postures to strengthen the adrenal glands are the safest and most natural cure of this condition.

soon became irritable, forgetful, and depressed. In time, they developed extreme fatigue, sleeplessness, heart palpitation, constipation and other digestive problems, neuritis, anemia, and low blood pressure. They suffered from severe headaches, nausea and vomiting, and were so exhausted they were unable to work.

Within a few hours after vitamin B1 was given to them, their fatigue and depression disappeared, and they became energetic, cheerful, and alert. Foods rich in this very important vitamin are: wheat germ, rice polish, nuts, dry beans, peas, soybeans, etc.

VITAMIN B12

Vitamin B12 is necessary for growth and blood formation, and for the maintenance of healthy nerve tissue. If this vitamin is lacking, especially if other B vitamins are also deficient, anemia may result. This is the only nutrient that plant foods cannot well supply, and so many doctors recommend that vegetarians take care to include enough vitamin B12 in their diet. The best source of vitamin B12 is milk (but it is also found in soy milk, wheat germ, and sea kelp). Milk is thus an essential food for vegetarians. The executive secretary of the U.S. National Academy of Sciences has said, "If you drink milk, many things are in your favor. Besides providing calcium, vitamin B12, and high-quality protein in its own right, milk can raise the value of other foods by adding some essential amino acids which they lack."

Even if you are not eating many B vitamins, your intestinal bacteria are probably synthesizing them for you. Cultured milk products such as yogurt of buttermilk will help you maintain a population of these beneficial bacteria. If for some reason you must take antibiotics, which often destroy the intestinal bacteria, afterwards you should eat plenty of yogurt to replace the bacteria, or take a Vitamin B supplement for a while.

VITAMIN C (ASCORBIC ACID)

Vitamin C is probably the most well-known of all the vitamins. It helps form the connective tissue which holds cells together and forms ligaments, cartilage, and the walls of the blood vessels. If vitamin C is lacking, the walls of the blood vessels become weak, allowing blood to flow into the tissues. As a result, the body bruises easily, the gums bleed, the teeth are susceptible to decay, and often there is pain in the joints as well. All these are danger signals of vitamin C deficiency. Indeed, many of the symptoms of old age—wrinkles, loose teeth, and brittle bones—are actually symptoms of vitamin C deficiency.

Ascorbic acid also facilitates the absorption and utilization of other nutrients, particularly iron; those who are anemic might be getting sufficient iron but not enough vitamin C to utilize it properly. Vitamin C concentrates in the lens of the eye, and so it is necessary for good vision; large doses of it can greatly improve eye infection and cataracts.

But the most important role of vitamin C seems to be as a detoxifier of the blood: it combines with any poison or toxic substance entering the body and eliminates it, thus purifying the body. Any foreign substance, even medicines, entering the blood, is more or less poisonous to the body; vitamin C eliminates the poison, but is itself destroyed in the process.* During infection and disease, the more vitamin C is given (sometimes even 20-40 times the normal amount), the more quickly the patient recovers. Countless infections and diseases have been studied, including meningitis, pneumonia, colds, eye infections, allergies, backache, and arthritis, and vitamin C has been found to alleviate them all.

Dr. Fred Klenner of the USA described dramatic success using vitamin C to treat patients seriously ill with meningitis, pneumonia, and other serious diseases. Huge amounts of antibiotics had been given to the patients without success, and their fevers had risen as high as 105 degrees. Within a few hours after vitamin C was injected, the fevers dropped and the patients' temperatures reached normal. In 2-3 days they were discharged from the hospital. Only a few minutes after the vitamin C was injected, no trace of it whatsoever could be found in the blood or the urine! Dr. Klenner believes that the vitamin combines immediately with the poisons or viruses, thus causing the fevers to drop.

When cloths wet with a vitamin C solution are laid over a patient with severe burns, most of the pain disappears and the burns heal rapidly. Chemical poisoning, snake and spider bites,

---

*Whenever strong allopathic drugs have to be taken, one should supply the body with enough Vitamin C at the same time to detoxify the drugs.

poison ivy and carbon monoxide poisoning have all been relieved when massive amounts of vitamin C were taken. Many doctors admit, "If anything should be called a miracle drug, it is vitamin C."

Vitamin C also seems to detoxify and eliminate the body's own toxic metabolic waste products (such as lactic acid) which cause fatigue, especially after extreme exertion. Experiments with soldiers showed that when soldiers carrying heavy equipment on long and difficult marches were given vitamin C, they experienced little fatigue, recovered quickly, and suffered no leg cramps. Those soldiers who were not given vitamin C suffered tremendous exhaustion and severe leg cramps, and did not recover for days. Thus many soldiers are given massive doses of vitamin C before going out on a difficult mission.

This effective vitamin is also useful to relieve mental stress; for extreme emotions, especially stressful negative ones, produce many toxins in the body. Persons with nervous or emotional disorders have been greatly relieved by taking vitamin C. Many doctors now recommend sufficient doses of vitamin C to those patients ho must undergo any stressful situation.

The best source of vitamin C is citrus fruits (oranges, lemons, grapefruits, tangerines, etc.). Green peppers have a high vitamin C content, and tomatoes and green vegetables are other good sources; but it is contained in almost all raw, fresh fruits and vegetables. Relatively small quantities of this vitamin are needed daily by the healthy person, and these amounts can very easily be obtained from natural sources without resorting to vitamin supplements. The minimum daily requirement is about 50 mg. or one glass of fresh orange juice or lemonade. Lemon juice with honey or salt is especially recommended to purify the body and relax the mind.

Vitamin C is a very delicate vitamin which is easily destroyed by heat, oxygen, light, and alkaline substances. Soon after a fruit is peeled or chopped, the vitamin C breaks down, so it is best to eat fruits and vegetables soon after they are cut. The effectiveness of vitamin C is also diminished by heat, processing and freezing. Since it is very soluble, the cooking water should always be used and not discarded.

38

Vitamin C content (per 100 gm):
Green peppers (raw) 128 mg.
Broccoli 90 mg.
Brussels sprouts 87 mg.   Turnip greens 69 mg.
Lemons 53 mg.   Oranges 61 mg.
Cabbage 53 mg.   Tomatoes 23 mg.
Grapefruit 38 mg.   Tangerines 31 mg.

VITAMIN D

Vitamin D is involved in the absorption of calcium, and is therefore important not only in bone formation but also for the proper functioning of the nerves. A lack of vitamin D can cause rickets and other bone diseases, tooth and gum decay, extreme nervousness and insomnia. Vitamin D can be formed on the skin by the contact of ultraviolet rays from the sun, and it is also plentifully supplied in milk and butter.

VITAMIN E

Vitamin E aids in the circulation of blood, and helps us conserve oxygen by preventing the fatty acids we eat from combining with oxygen and thus wasting it. If vitamin E is lacking, the oxygen in our cells is continuously wasted, and thus the body's need for it tremendously increases. Athletes and mountain climbers who get plenty of vitamin E have much more endurance than those who lack it. It is especially valuable in illnesses where the oxygen supply is limited, such as asthma and emphysema. This vitamin also helps the body heal without scarring, which occurs when the tissues are deprived of sufficient oxygen; it can prevent pain and scarring from even very serious burns. It also aids in the circulation of the blood, and helps to dissolve bloodclots in the vessels, thus preventing heart attacks and varicose veins. Vitamin E is necessary for strong muscles and good posture, and pregnant mothers who lack it usually have babies with very weak muscles who have difficulty learning to walk. Lack of sufficient vitamin E has been found to be a major cause of premature babies.

Vitamin E is found in the oils of all beans, nuts, and seeds, but much of its value is lost by frying. Soybean oil is wonderfully rich in vitamin E; other good sources are nuts, wheat germ, peas and beans, green leaves, sweet potatoes and butter:

Vitamin E content (per 100 gm.):
Soybean oil 14 mg.
Sweet potatoes 3.6 mg.
Beans & peas 2.4 mg.
Butter 2 mg.
Turnip greens 2 mg.

WHAT IS THE "VITAL LIFE" PRINCIPLE?

The Vital Life Principle states that certain foods contain more life force (*prana*) than others. The importance of vitality in foods was appreciated 2500 years ago by Pythagoras, who said, "Only living, fresh foods can enable human beings to apprehend the truth."

We know that all life lives on energy from the sun, and this energy is stored inside green plants, fruits, nuts, grains, and vegetables. When we eat these, we consume the solar energy directly. In other words, we feed on "live" food with almost all the vital energy still intact. Many plants retain their life-giving energy for many days after they are picked; in fact, they remain still capable of sprouting and growing. By the time meat is consumed, however, it has already been in the process of decay for several days.

So when we eat meat, we swallow "dead food"—food from which the vital energy has mostly decayed.

For thousands of years yogis and sages have taught that both body and mind are profoundly influenced by what we eat. According to spiritual teacher P. R. Sarkar, "The human body is constituted of innumerable living cells. The nature of your living cells will be formed in accordance with the type of food you take, and ultimately this will affect your mind to some extent. If the cells of the human body grow on food, rotten and bad-smelling from the flesh of animals in which mean tendencies predominate, it is but natural that the mind will lean more towards meanness."

Actually, the word "vegetarian" does not come from "vegetable" but rather from the Latin word *vegetare* which means "to enliven." When the Romans used the term *homo vegetus*, they did not mean a vegetable-eater, but a vigorous and dynamically healthy person.

WHAT TO EAT: NUTRITIOUS FOODS

To maximize the nutritional value of your diet, as much as possible try to eat:

Raw foods full of vital energy
The closer a food is to its natural state, the greater its nutritional value. Many vitamins and essential nutrients are completely or partially destroyed by cooking, especially excess cooking. Raw foods are full of vital energy (*prana*). Actually we are eating food only to obtain this very prana in our bodies, so it makes sense to eat foods which possess as much of this life-giving vital energy as possible. Ancient sages used to live completely on raw fruits, nuts and roots from the jungles and mountains, and they lived long and healthy lives. So whenever possible, try to eat food in its natural state, as fresh as possible—plenty of fresh fruits and salads every day. Freshly sprouted seeds, beans and grains are ideal foods, full of vital energy. Reduce the amount of processed and preserved, boxed and bottled, canned and pickled foods you eat—they often have many harmful chemicals and preservatives added to prevent their spoilage. (Sugared bottled drinks such as colas are especially bad for health.)

And when you cook, do not overcook the food—the prana and vitamins are lost by long heating. Steamed vegetables are preferable to boiling; but if you do cook vegetables in water, drink the juices, don't discard them. Chinese-style wok-cooking is excellent because the vegetables are cooked quickly and much of their nutritional value is retained.

Whole grains & unrefined foods
White rice and white flour, and especially white sugar, have very little food value as compared with brown rice, whole wheat flour and wheat germ, molasses and honey.

Sufficient protein—but not too much
Don't worry needlessly about protein; if you drink a glass of milk every day, or eat soybean products, beans or nuts, and eat plenty of fresh vegetables, your body is getting all the protein it needs. In fact, too much protein will make the body acidic, and many sick-

nesses may result. Wheat germ is excellent for health because it not only contains protein but is also a superior source of the B vitamins which help the body to utilize protein efficiently. (Raw wheat germ is most nutritious but requires cold storage.)

Not much sugar, fatty and oily foods

These are highly acidic and may create over-acidity in the body, the cause of many diseases. Whenever possible, substitute honey or molasses for sugar, and boil, bake or steam vegetables instead of frying.

HOW TO EAT: EATING HABITS

1 Do not overeat

Doctors repeatedly warn us not to overeat, for overeating stresses the entire digestive system and prevents the proper digestion of food. The half-digested food then forms a putrid, decaying mass in the body and poisons our blood stream, and ultimately weakens the entire system (see page 115). According to yogic science, no matter how healthy or pure a food is, when an excess is consumed it automatically becomes of the "static" type, crudifying to the body and mind. So yogis have always advised to fill the stomach 1/2 with food, 1/4 with water, and 1/4 with air.

Stop eating while you are still hungry; you will feel full as soon as the sugars and other nutrients have time to enter the bloodstream and affect the brain.

2 Eat in a peaceful and joyous mood

Actually, how you eat is as important as what you eat. If you eat hurriedly, or in a tired, disturbed, or unhappy state of mind, your food will not be digested properly and all its nutrition will be lost. When the mind is upset, the entire body becomes upset as well. Photographs of the stomachs of individuals in a state of anger show the stomach to be swollen, rigid and red, with no pliability of natural peristaltic motion. Obviously indigestion is impossible in such a state of mind and body. When we eat in a disturbed mood, not only is the food not digested properly, but this undigested food produces very harmful acids and toxins in our body—it would have been better not to have eaten at all.

For this reason you should try to eat as much as possible in a peaceful mood, in serene and happy surroundings; avoid noisy and unpleasant restaurants. It is advisable to pause in silence for a moment before eating to calm the mind and remember that the food is actually, in its essence, pure consciousness. Then eat with others in a joyous atmosphere, and remember—laughter aids digestion!

3 Do not eat too many varieties of foods

Forcing the digestive system to digest many different types of foods also strains and weakens it. For this reason, it is advisable to eat no more than four different preparations of food at one meal. Try to keep your meals as simple as possible, and avoid eating too much spicy food.

4 Chew your food thoroughly

Especially starches like rice, bread, noodles, etc., whose digestion actually starts in the mouth, where the saliva must mix thoroughly with it to prepare it for the stomach. Chew carefully; do not bolt your food hurriedly down your throat, or it will pass undigested into the stomach and release toxins which will weaken the entire digestive system. (The saliva is highly alkaline and so if it is mixed well with the food, it can help neutralize the ill-effects of acidic foods.)

5 Sit in proper posture while eating

Sit with your back straight, so the energy can flow freely along the spine and there is no pressure on the digestive organs. Actually the best posture for digestion is sitting cross-legged; in India where people have traditionally eaten in this posture for centuries, it is called *bhojanasana* or "food posture." Never eat or drink standing up.

6 Try to rest after meals and keep your right nostril open

Do not engage in any strenuous physical or mental activity after meals. At this time, all the body's energy and blood is needed in the digestive organs, and directing it to the muscles for physical labor or to the brain for concentrated thought will reduce one's mental and physical efficiency and impair digestion as well.

There are two main subtle energy channels in the body (called *Ida* and *Piungala* in Sanskrit) which weave around the spinal column and end in each nostril. When the breath is flowing predominantly through the left nostril, the body remains cool; subtle, spiritual energy is flowing through the body and the mind is elevated to a subtler, more spiritual state of consciousness. This is the most conducive time for profound thought or meditation.

When the breath is flowing predominantly through the right nostril, the body is more heated and the mind and the body are prepared for physical activity in the material world. Because the body needs heat for indigestion, the right nostril should always be open during and after meals. If at mealtime the right nostril is closed and the left one open, it is better not to take solid, heavy foods because they will be more difficult to digest; liquids and light foods are best at these time. After a meal, to keep the breath flowing through the right nostril, it is advisable to lay on your left side: this automatically opens the right nostril.

7 Avoid eating between meals

It takes about four hours for the food to leave your stomach and for the digestive juices to accumulate again, ready to digest the next meal. If you eat many times a day, the digestive juices never have a chance to accumulate to their full strength, and then these weakened juices cannot digest the food properly. Thus it is best to eat only when you are really hungry (never when your stomach is already full), and not more than four times a day.

8 Do not eat too late at night, too close to bedtime

It is best to eat about one to 1 1/2 hours before bedtime, otherwise the heat of digestion will produce gases which will affect the brain and cause many disturbing dreams. Walking in the open air before retiring will help digest the food and relax you before sleep. If you have trouble sleeping at night, drink a glass of warm milk before bed.

9 Drink plenty of water every day

Water is nature's cleanser which keeps the body pure and free from poisons and waste. A healthy person should drink about three to four liters of water or other liquids a day; a diseased person, especially one with skin disease, should drink four to five liters. (If you are not accustomed to drinking much water, do not start drinking so much all at once; rather gradually increase your daily intake). Drink a little bit at a time, a 1/2 glass or a glass, many times a day, but not too much with meals, otherwise the digestive juices will be too diluted and digestion impaired. Add a little lemon and salt (or honey) to the water you drink.

10 Do not eat very hot or very cold foods

Too hot foods will overheat the body and interfere with the action of the digestive enzymes, many of which can function only within a limited range of temperature. They may damage the mucous membranes which line the digestive tract as well.

Let the food cool a little before eating. Too cold foods and beverages, on the other hand, constrict the intestinal canal, making digestion more difficult, and also harmfully affect the throat. Cold foods may constrict the delicate respiratory tubes leading from the nose into the lungs, making them more sensitive: Sometimes the shock of drinking cold drinks can trigger an attack of asthma or other allergy.

11 Get plenty of fresh air and exercise

The body needs exercise to stimulate and strengthen the digestive organs and facilitate digestion, and the fires of digestion need plenty of oxygen "fuel." If your body is sluggish and lazy, your digestion and overall health will suffer. One of the best cures for constipation is to get plenty of exercise every day: at least go for a daily walk in the open air.

12 Do "half-bath" before every meal

The body produces much heat during and after meals, so it should first be cooled before eating. Before each meal, (as well as before meditation, yoga exercises, and sleep) you should do "half-bath":

1—Pour cool water on the genital area
2—On the legs from the knees down
3—On the arms from the elbows down
4—Holding water in the mouth, splash water on the open eyes, 12 times
5—Pull water through the nostrils and spit it out the mouth, 3 times
6—Wash the ears with the forefingers, and behind the ears
7—Wash behind the neck
This practice also calms the heart, and is very relaxing to the mind and body. If practiced regularly, it is excellent for health.

13 Do *utksepa mudra* every morning to avoid constipation

Constipation and poor digestion are actually the cause of most diseases. To keep the digestive system clean and clear, do the following yoga exercise every morning before arising from bed.

While lying down, inhale and bend your legs and press your knees up firmly against your chest, and hold your breath in this position for a few moments. Then vigorously straighten the legs again, while exhaling. Repeat 4 times. This exercise stimulates the peristaltic motion of the digestive system which has become slow and sluggish during sleep and thus prevents constipation. Then rise briskly from bed, and immediately drink a glass of water (you might want to keep a glass of water beside your bed at night), or lemon water with a little honey or salt. Doctors have found that drinking liquid on an empty stomach immediately upon arising quickly washes wastes out of the system and promotes digestion. Do not touch the water to your teeth as you drink; this would wash back into you stomach all the toxins which have collected overnight on your teeth. Then, uncovering the navel, walk about the room for about five minutes, with the navel area uncovered. This vitalizes and strengthens the solar plexus (*manipura cakra*) which controls heat and digestion, by exposing it to the fresh morning air.

14 Try to eat food cooked by sentient people

Not only does the state of your own mind and your environment affect your food and its digestion, but also the way it is cooked. Everyone who touches your food leaves the invisible imprint of their vibration on it, and the more sensitive you are, the more it will affect you. Try to eat foods cooked by pure and loving people, and when you are preparing food for others, keep your own thoughts happy and pure—and sing elevating songs while you cook!

"If anyone invites you with sincere cordiality to dinner, you should gladly accept even if they entertain you with only boiled vegetables and rice; but if anyone invites you to dinner just to make a show of their wealth, you should never take food there."
                                                    —P.R. Sarkar

FOOD IS YOUR BEST MEDICINE

"Your foods shall be your remedies, and your remedies shall be your foods."
                          —Hippocrates, the "Father of Medicine"

In reality, disease is not caused by virus and bacteria, microscopic monsters of external origin, which invade our bodies like an army of tiny devils. These viruses and bacteria are all around us, and within our bodies at all times—why then do we fall victim to them and become sick at certain times and not at others, and why do some people get affected, and not others? The answer is simple: all disease starts from inside our bodies and minds, caused by wrong thinking, wrong living, and wrong eating. If we live naturally, in accordance with the laws of the harmony of the universe, we will not fall sick in mind or body. It is only when we disobey these natural universal laws that illness results—a warning signal for us to retrieve our lost harmony with nature. When our bodies are filled with poisons and putrifying waste materials, they become weak and unable to resist the attack of bacteria and virus, and various diseases appear. Thus the root cause of all disease is not the external agents of bacteria and virus, but the impurities in our own bodies caused by improper digestion and elimination.

Alkalinity & acidity
In its natural state, the body is slightly alkaline, with a pH of 7.4. In this condition the chemical processes of the body can function

most efficiently and all the waste products of these processes are rapidly eliminated. However, if too much acidic food is eaten, and the body and blood become acidic instead of alkaline; the spleen, liver, heart, and kidneys, which are the blood-purifying organs, become overworked and ultimately weakened and susceptible to disease. Then the waste poisons can no longer be properly eliminated, and instead collect in the joints, causing rheumatism and gout; or seek elimination through the skin, causing eczema, acne, sores and boils. The condition of acidity thus may be a contributing factor to many different diseases, including piles, cancer, leprosy, paralysis, kidney and liver trouble, gall bladder stones and infections, tuberculosis, impotency, high blood pressure and heart disease, strokes and heart attack, asthma and other allergies, etc. The treatment for the acid condition of the body, and thus the remedy for many diseases, is to minimize the amount of acidic food eaten, and increase the amount of alkaline food.

"Never let the fruits, roots and vegetable soups (alkaline foods) you eat be less than the quantity of acidic and starchy foods—the less acidic food, the better."
     —*Yogic Treatment & Natural Remedies* by P. R. Sarkar

Acid foods
The acid-producing foods which should be avoided in cases of indigestion and ill health are:

✗ Meats, fish & eggs
✗ Tea, coffee & alcohol
✗ Condiments, pickles, sauces & vinegar
✗ Starches & grains, especially white, refined starches, rice, bread, noodles, crackers, cereals, etc.)
✗ Spices
✗ Onions, garlic, & mushrooms
✗ Most beans (including kidney beans, peas & lentils)
✗ Some nuts, such as peanuts & walnuts
✗ Oils & all fatty & fried foods
✗ Sugary foods, especially white sugar & its products: jam, jelly, syrup, candies, sweets, pastries, ice cream, canned fruits & soft drinks (highly acidic and quickly erode the teeth).

Certain grains can be made less acidic by cooking or preparing them properly. For instance, if bread is toasted, its starch changes into fructose or "fruit sugar", the same easily-digestible carbohydrate which is found in fruits. Thus toast is more alkaline and digestible than plain bread, and so it is preferable in case of disease. Similarly, if white rice is soaked in water for about 30 seconds before eating, much of the acidic starch is washed off and it is not so harmful to the body. Many whole grains (brown rice, rice powder, brown bread, wheat germ, etc.) are much less acidic than the white, refined grains, and should be substituted whenever possible.

Many doctors recommend avoiding chocolate also, because it contains cocoa butter, a very heavy and hard-to-digest fat which causes constipation and skin eruption.

Alkaline foods
The alkaline foods, which should be increased in the diet are:

✓ Almost all vegetables, especially green leafy vegetables, & soups made of these vegetables. Sprouts, especially, are excellent cleansers for the body, & are full of vitamins and minerals. Among all the beans, soy beans are the most alkaline—an excellent treatment for over-acidity.
✓ Milk, butter & especially buttermilk.
✓ Honey & molasses
✓ Most nuts, such as almonds, Brazil nuts, chestnuts, hazel nuts.
✓ Fruits & fruit juices, especially juicy fruits: they are among the easiest foods to digest, since they can be digested in their own fluids & the organs do not have to make much effort to digest them.

Nutrition experts call fruits the "best alkalinzer and internal cleanser known," and "the most natural remedy."

—PAPAYA contains an enzyme called papain, a digestive aid, and is thus very good for the stomach.
—APPLES are very rich in potassium, which helps neutralize the toxins in the mouth, and thus they are excellent teeth and gum

cleansers.

—FIGS have a special enzyme called ficin which dissolves poisons in the bloodstream, and also contain seratonin which is thought to strengthen and improve the mind. The ancient scholars and sages of the Middle East used to fast for many days eating only figs and water to attain superior mental power.

—PINEAPPLES contain bromelin which cleanses the pancreas.

—TOMATOES are highly alkaline and are good neutralizers of acidity.

—BANANAS contain a good deal of potassium which is good for the nerves, and so they are an excellent tonic for nervous depression when it is related to potassium deficiency. They are especially nutritious when taken with milk.

—COCONUT is a very alkaline food; coconut water or milk is an excellent treatment for any disease caused by acidity. Shredded coconut mixed with anise seed is another.

—APRICOTS are an excellent source of vitamin A and iron.

—LEMONS are highly alkaline and for this reason lemon juice is prescribed by yogis as an excellent medicine for almost all diseases. Drink lemon water all day, small quantities at a time. It is best if you add a little salt or honey. (Although lemon and other citrus fruits are themselves acidic, they produce an alkaline reaction during digestion.) ORANGES are also very cleansing and have a high vitamin C content.

—BERRIES such as raspberries, strawberries, gooseberries, currants, etc. are alkaline if eaten quite ripe, otherwise they are acidic.

SPECIFIC DISEASES

The nutritional treatment for several common diseases is described below. For more information about the herbal and exercise treatment for these diseases and many others as well, please consult *Yogic Treatments and Natural Remedies*, by P. R. Sarkar (Calcutta, 1983).

DYSPEPSIA

Dyspepsia or indigestion is caused by over-acidity in the blood, as described above. When this over-acidity weakens the digestive organs so much that they can no longer function efficiently, the half-digested food is not converted into a soluble liquid but instead decays or ferments in the intestines and partially blocks them, causing constipation. As a result, a poisonous and fetid gas is produced, which causes belching, distension of the abdominal area, loss of appetite, offensive gas, physical weakness, and extreme irritability. As a result of dyspepsia, many more serious diseases may arise, such as ulcers, boils, dysentery, and even tuberculosis.

The best food remedy for dyspepsia is to completely eliminate non-vegetarian foods and intoxicants from the diet, which are poisons for dyspepsia patients. Rather the soup of green vegetables and yogurt mixed with water and a little salt should be taken. Shredded dry coconut mixed with anise seed is also helpful in this disease. Eating when not hungry or only slightly hungry is very harmful, as is eating rich foods. One should take rest after meals and avoid overeating; the general rule is to fill the stomach halfway with food, one-quarter with water, and to keep one-quarter empty.

It is best to avoid breakfast, but if one feels very hungry, sweet or juicy fruits can be taken, especially mango, pineapple, citrus fruits or papaya. It is best to eat dinner before 8 p.m., and take a short walk afterwards; and meals should always be taken when the breath is flowing through the right nostril. Fasting twice a month is also desirable. It is essential to take a walk daily in the fresh air, and do a little physical labor every day.

RHEUMATISM

Excess acidity is also the main cause of this disease and the primary treatment is to minimize the amount of acidic food taken. If 3/4 of the food eaten is alkaline, it will cure rheumatism completely within a very short time. Rheumatism patients should drink 4-5 liters of water a day, a little at a time, and eat plenty of sweet and sour fruits and roots. Fasting twice a month is also beneficial.

EMACIATION IN CHILDREN

Surprisingly, emaciation in children is not only due to poverty or malnourishment, but also due to over-feeding children. Some misguided parents feed their children non-vegetarian foods such as eggs, fish and meat from babyhood; as a result, the livers and other digestive organs of the children are overworked and weakened, and the children become thin.

The main food of children under five should be milk, fruits and root vegetables. The less carbohydrates and fatty foods children are fed the better, because such foods weaken the undeveloped livers and digestive organs of children. Under no circumstances should children under 5 years be fed non-vegetarian food. From that age on, starches and fatty foods may be given in gradually increasing amounts; but fruits, roots and all kinds of alkaline foods are always the best diet for children. If children get enough of this type of food, their emaciation will be completely cured.

ULCER

When due to over-acidity or weakness of the digestive organs, undigested, fermented food accumulates in the duodenum, the excess acidity may cause gastric and duodenal ulcers in the lining of the intestines. Since acidity is the main cause of this disease (other contributing causes may be excessive mental anxiety coupled with a lack of physical exercise, or the use of strong medicines), acidic foods should be carefully avoided, especially non-vegetarian food and all types of intoxicants, as well as very sweet, spicy and salty foods. All ulcer patients must take daily at least 2 or 3 spoonfuls of honey mixed with water or milk, and be sure to rest after meals before doing any physical or mental work. Those with ulcers should never eat much at a time but rather eat several times a day, a small quantity each time. The cure of this disease depends largely on diet. (See *Yogic Treatments & Natural Remedies* for more detailed instructions.)

OBESITY

Those who suffer from obesity are generally those who get little physical exercise but eat large quantities of high-calorie foods, sweets, and non-vegetarian foods. When this fat is stored in the abdominal region, it may cause sterility in women and impotency in men, which is why many obese people have no children. As they grow older and their livers become weak, they begin to suffer from acidity, constipation or intestinal troubles, difficulty in respiration and high blood pressure.

Some obese people merely try to eat less to lose weight, but this is an incorrect approach because such dieting may greatly weaken them. Rather they should follow a simple, carefully selected diet, for instance:

1) Drinking 4-5 liters of water daily, a little at a time, preferably mixed with lemon juice and salt.
2) Avoiding non-vegetarian and fried foods completely.
3) Drinking 3/4-1 liter diluted milk daily, a little at a time.
4) Eating plenty of fruits, especially sour juicy fruits.
5) Reducing or eliminating from the diet grains and beans, and instead eating plenty of green vegetables and vegetable soups.
6) Reducing the use of sugar and substituting honey instead (but not more than 3 spoonfuls per day).
7) Fasting twice a month.
8) Getting plenty of exercise (there are specific yoga exercises for obesity; see *Yogic Treatments and Natural Remedies*).

IS THERE ANY CONNECTION BETWEEN OUR MEAT-EATING HABITS AND WORLD STARVATION?

Yes!

If we conserved our grain supply and gave it to the poor and malnourished, instead of to cattle, we could easily feed nearly all of the chronically underfed people of the world.

If we ate half as much meat, we could release enough food to feed the entire "developing world."

A Harvard nutritionist, Jean Mayer, estimates that reducing meat production by just 10% would release enough grain to feed 60 million people.

The shocking and tragic truth is that 80-90% of all grain grown in America is used to feed meat animals.

Twenty years ago, the average American ate 50 pounds of meat annually; this year he will eat 129 pounds of beef alone. Because of America's "fixation on meat," most eat twice the daily recommended protein allowance. Learning the real facts behind the "food shortage" is fundamental to an understanding of how we can properly utilize the world's resources.

More and more scientists and world economists are strongly advocating a vegetarian diet to solve the tremendous food problems of our planet, because, they say, eating meat is one of the main causes of these problems.

But how does vegetarianism relate to food shortage?

The answer is simple: meat is the most uneconomical and inefficient food we can eat; the cost of one pound of meat protein is twenty times higher than equally nutritional plant protein. Only 10% of the protein and calories we feed to our livestock is recovered in the meat we eat; that is, 90% goes "down the drain."

Vast acres of land are used to raise livestock for food. These acres of land could be utilized far more productively if planted with grains, beans, and other legumes for humans to eat directly. For example, one acre used to raise a steer will provide only about one pound of protein; but this same land planted with soybeans will produce 17 pounds of protein! In other words, to eat meat, we need to use 17 times as much land as the amount needed to plant soybeans. In addition, soybeans are more nutritious, contain less fat, and are free from the poisons of meat.

Raising animals for food is a tremendous waste of the world's resources not only of land, but also of water. It is estimated that raising food for a meat diet uses eight times as much water as growing vegetables and grains.

This means that while millions of people all over the world are starving, a few rich people are wasting vast amounts of land, water, and grain in order to eat meat, which is slowly destroying their bodies. Americans consume over a ton of grain per person per year (through feed for meat-producing livestock), while the rest of the world averages about 400 pounds of grain.

United Nations Secretary General Kurt Waldheim has said that the food consumption of the rich countries is the key cause of the hunger around the world, and the United Nations has strongly recommended that these countries cut down on their meat consumption.

The primary solution to the global food crisis, many scientists are saying, is to gradually convert from a meat diet to a vegetarian diet. "If we were vegetarians, we could banish hunger from this earth. Children would be born and grow up well-nourished, and they would live happier, healthier lives. Animals would be free to live as wild, natural creatures, not forced to reproduce in great numbers as slaves to be fattened for the slaughter, with food that hungry people should be eating." (B. Pinkus, *Vegetable Based Proteins*).

Because many scientists are saying that the bulk of future food needs will be met by plant proteins, several Western countries are currently financing much research to develop delicious, vegetable-based proteins made from soy flour. But the people of Asia, among others, are way ahead of even this high level of research; they have been obtaining excellent protein by eating tofu and other soy products for thousands of years.

The vegetarian diet is the diet of the future—the diet which we human beings must adopt once again if we are to save our natural resources and, even more important, the precious lives of human beings all over the world. The vegetarian today is the human being of the future. Today's vegetarian points toward the direction that everyone will eventually follow, as people realize more and more the benefits of eating a vegetarian diet and the disastrous results of pursuing our present course.

Although meat production is surely a major contributor to the global food crisis, it is only a graphic representation of the underlying problem: an obscured yet pervasive pattern which permeates every aspect of the struggle to obtain basic needs of everyone on our planet.

"The earth has enough for everyone's need, but not enough for everyone's greed."

—Mahatma Gandhi

THE POLITICS OF HUNGER

According to a widely accepted myth about world hunger, the world does not have the capacity to feed its people. Everyone is doing the best they can, so the story goes. "There is simply not enough to go around. The hungry masses are rapidly multiplying, and if we are to avert disaster, a concerted effort to control population must be vigorously pursued."

However, a rapidly growing number of renowned scientists, economists, and agricultural experts are expressing their strong disagreement with this. "It is patently false—a myth," they say. "Actually there IS enough to go around, and then some. Any scarcities are due to wasteful utilization of resources and their irrational distribution."

According to Buckminster Fuller, there are enough resources at present to feed, clothe, house, and educate every human being on the planet at American middle class standards! Recent research by the Institute for Food and Development Policy has shown that there is no country in the world in which the people could not feed themselves from their own resources. There is no correlation between land density and hunger, they say. India is usually cited as the classic example of what happens when overpopulation occurs, and yet China has twice as many people per cultivated acre as India, and in China people are not hungry. Bangladesh has just one-half the people per cultivated acre that Taiwan has, yet Taiwan has no starvation while Bangladesh has one of the highest rates in the world. In fact, the most densely populated countries in the world today are NOT India and Bangladesh, but Holland and Japan. Clearly, population density is not the reason people starve. Of course the world can reach a limit of being able to support human population, but this limit is estimated to be about 40 billion (we are currently at 4 billion). Today more than half the world's people are hungry all the time; nearly half are starving. If there is enough to go around, where is it?

Let us take a look at who controls food and how it is controlled. The food industry is the largest in the world—to the tune of $150 billion a year (larger than auto, steel, or oil industries). A relatively few, giant multinational corporations dominate the industry; concentration of power is in their hands. It has become generally recognized and been well documented that giant corporations hold extensive political control; what this means is that a relatively few corporations are in a position to regulate and control the flow of food to billions of people. How is this possible?

One of the ways giant corporations are able to control the market is gradually to take over every phase of the food system. For example, one giant corporation will produce farm machinery, feed, fertilizers, fuel, food containers; it will buy chains of supermarkets, wholesale businesses, and processing plants, and grow the food. A small farmer cannot compete with this because the corporation can artificially lower prices to undercut competition and drive the small farmer out of business and then it more than recovers its losses by artificially raising the prices in areas where it has destroyed the competition. Thus we see that since World War II the number of farms in the U.S.A. has dropped by half; more than 1,000 independent farmers are leaving their farms every week. And yet a U.S. Department of Agriculture study has recently shown that small, independent farms can produce food much more cheaply and efficiently than the giant agribusiness farms!

Sheer economic strength: in the U.S., for example, less than one-tenth of one percent of all corporations own over 50% of all the corporate wealth. For instance, 90% of all grain marketing is controlled by only six companies. Power of decision: agribusiness corporations decide what crops are to be produced, how much, what quality, and what price they are to be sold for. They have the power to hold back production or to store huge supplies of food, thereby creating artificial scarcities (which are notorious for raising prices).

Governmental agencies that are supposed to regulate such matters are themselves dominated by agribusiness policy. Top governmental positions (Secretary of Agriculture, etc.) are regularly held by agribusiness' top corporation executives.

Multinational giants have been extremely successful in achieving their goal of maximizing profits and amassing wealth. The rule of thumb is to increase prices as much as possible, while keeping production at the minimum necessary to sell the goods, so that in the short run prices fluctuate, but on a long range basis they only rise fairly rapidly.

Multinationals are buying more and more land. A study of 83 countries revealed that just over 3% of land holders control about 80% of the farmland.

Although this pattern has meant huge profits for a few, it has been a great detriment to many. There is no "land scarcity" or "food shortage" actually. If the goal were to utilize the resources of the world to meet humanity's needs, the goal could and would be easily met.

However, with a goal of maximum profits for a few, we have the tragic situation of a planet with half its people hungry. Truly speaking, the aspiration to become rich by exploiting others is a sort of mental malady—an ailment that leads to all sorts of distortions on our earth.

In Central America, where over 70% of the children are hungry, 50% of the land is used for "cash crops" (crops, such as lilies, which yield fast, big profits but are of little use for human survival). While multinational corporations use the best land to grow their cash crops (coffee, tea, tobacco, exotic foods), the local people are forced to use slopes and eroded land on which it is difficult to grow food.

Development funds have irrigated the desert in Senegal so that multinational firms can grow eggplant and mangoes for airfreighting to Europe's best tables.

In Haiti the majority of (utterly impoverished) peasants struggle for survival by trying to grow food on mountain slopes of a 45 degree incline or more. They say they are exiles from their birthright—some of the world's richest agricultural land. These lands now belong to a handful of elite; cattle are flown in by U.S. firms for grazing and re-exported to franchised hamburger restaurants.

In Mexico, land that was once used for growing corn for Mexicans is now used for the production of fancy vegetables for U.S. citizens; the profit is 20 times greater. Hundreds of thousands of former farmers have found themselves landless. Unable to compete with large landowners, they first lease their land to make at least some money from it; the next step is to work for the big firms; finally they find themselves migrant workers, roaming in search of work so their families can survive. Such conditions have led to repeated waves of rebellion.

In 1975, Colombia's best soil was used to produce 18 million dollars of flowers. Carnations brought 80 times greater profit than did the former crop, wheat.

Not enough to go around? Hardly. The good land, the best resource, is being used to produce luxury crops for profit. Throughout much of the world we find a consistent, pervasive pattern. Agriculture, once the livelihood of millions of self-supporting farmers, is being turned into the production sites of high-profit non-essentials for the (well-fed) minority who can pay. Contrary to widespread myths, our food security is not being threatened by the prolific, hungry masses but by elites that profit by the concentration and internationalization of control of food resources.

Meat production is the epitome of this pervasive system. "The poor man's grain is being siphoned to feed the rich man's cow," says the director of the United Nations Protein Advisory group. As the demand for meat increases, rich nations are buying more and more grain to feed pigs and cattle. Grain supplies, once used to feed people, are sold to the highest bidder, and countless human beings are effectively condemned to starvation. "The wealthy can compete for the poor man's food; the poor cannot compete at all."

In a "Final Note to Consumers," John Powell of Food Education for Action writes: "The price of food will probably go up this summer, despite the fact that the price of grain has dropped 50% since 1973, which your food bill has not yet reflected. But, in looking for the reasons for this increase, don't just look at Arabs and the price of oil and booming population in the Third World. Look to the multinational corporations that control food industry with a little help from their friends in government. And remember, they are in the business of making money, not feeding people. And while we are trying to explode myths, let's remember we are not helpless."

"When the whole property of this universe has been inherited by all creatures, how can there be any justification for a system in which someone receives a flow of huge excess, while others die for lack of a handful of grains?"

—P.R. Sarkar

Indeed we are not helpless. And even though the difficulties facing humanity may seem almost insurmountable, many people feel that we are at the threshold of a new era, when human beings everywhere will recognize the simple truth that human society is One and indivisible; thus the suffering of one implies the suffering of all.

In discussing how a society based on universalism can be established, P. R. Sarkar explains:

"A harmonious society can be achieved by mobilizing the living spirit of those who desire to establish one human society... those at the forefront of such a moral movement will be leaders of moral integrity, leaders whose goal is not fame or wealth or power but the interests of the whole human society."

"Just as the advent of the crimson dawn is inevitable at the end of the cimmerian darkness of the interlunar night, exactly in the same way I know that a gloriously brilliant chapter will also come after the endless reproach and humiliation of the neglected humanity of today. Those who love humanity, those who desire the welfare of all living beings, should be vigorously active from this very moment, after shaking off all lethargy and sloth, so that the most auspicious hour arrives at the earliest."

"...This endeavor, the well-being of the human race, concerns everyone—it is yours, mine, and ours. We may afford to ignore our rights, but we must not forget our responsibilities. Forgetting our responsibilities implies the humiliation of the human race."

AHIMSA: NON-INJURY TO LIVING BEINGS

Once the great Russian writer, Leo Tolstoy, had a dinner party at his home. He was a vegetarian and almost all of his guests were also, except one lady. When she sat down to eat, she found, to her amazement, that there was nothing on her plate, and a live chicken tied to her chair! Tolstoy explained, "My conscience forbids me to kill the chicken. Since you are the only guest eating meat, I would be greatly obliged if you would undertake the killing first."

All the aforementioned practical considerations (health, economy, etc.) are not the only reasons for not eating meat. One of the most important reasons is that we should not take life, even animal life, unnecessarily. Many religious and spiritual groups have advocated a vegetarian diet, because of the sacredness of all life and the need to live without causing suffering. According to their view, a true human being views animals not as slaves and food, but as younger brothers and sisters, and feels we have no right to cause them agony and brutally take their lives unless our survival absolutely depends upon it. Since it is possible for us to live more healthy lives without ever eating meat, it is appropriate to ask whether meat eating is a moral and humane habit. Clearly animals do not give up their lives willingly so that we can have the luxury of eating their flesh.

Anyone who has visited a slaughter house can testify to the fact that animals suffer greatly before and during their slaughter. In the United States alone nearly 9 million creatures are slaughtered daily for supposed dietary needs. Those of us who would weep if our dog or cat were killed go on silently condoning the needless slaughter of millions of animals each day.

P. R. Sarkar, explains *ahimsa* in this way: "As far as possible, articles of food are to be selected from amongst the sets of items where development of consciousness is comparatively little, i.e., if vegetables are available, animals should not be slaughtered. Secondly, before killing any animal having developed or underdeveloped consciousness, consider over and over whether it is possible to live in a healthy body without taking such lives."

Many other great saints have shared this view. During the early days of the Christian movement, for example, a large number of Christian and Jewish sects opposed meat eating as a costly and cruel luxury. Throughout history wise people and spiritual leaders have counseled that we will never be able to evolve to higher states of consciousness or create a human society based on love, until we give up the brutal habit of eating meat:

"It is my view that the vegetarian manner of living, by its purely physical effect on the human temperament, would most beneficially influence the lot of mankind."

—Albert Einstein

"Truly man is the kind of beasts, for his brutality exceeds them. We live by the death of others. We are burial places! I have since an early age abjured the use of meat, and the time will come when people will look upon the murder of animals as they now look upon the murder of human beings."

—Leonardo da Vinci

"This is dreadful! Not only the suffering and death of the animals, but by eating meat man suppresses in himself, unnecessarily, the highest spiritual capacity—that of sympathy and pity towards living creatures like himself—and by violating his own feelings, becomes cruel."

—**Leo Tolstoy**

"World peace, or any other kind of peace, depends greatly on the attitude of the mind. Vegetarianism can bring about the right mental attitude for peace... it holds forth a better way of life, which, if practiced universally, can lead to a better, more just, and more peaceful community of nations."

—**U Nu, former Prime Minister of Burma**

"While we ourselves are the living graves of murdered animals, how can we expect any ideal conditions on the earth?"

—**George Bernard Shaw**

I STILL LIKE THE TASTE OF MEAT —WHAT SHALL I DO?

An ancient yogic principle suggests that the best way to change a deeply embedded habit is NOT to "pull it out by the roots" (a nearly impossible task), but rather to plant, nurture and cultivate an opposing habit next to the old one—and to give the new habit a lot of care, love and attention. Very soon this new habit will grow strong and beautiful, and, with hardly an effort, the old weed, i.e., the flesh-eating habit, will wither and drop out of sight.

The task of changing from a carnivorous diet to a diet of living, fresh, nutritious foods is much easier than it might initially seem. There are literally thousands of highly nutritious, tasty dishes non-vegetarians have never had the opportunity to sample due to habit, conditioning, and lack of information. Most people are astonished to discover so many high protein dishes made from ingredients they are totally unfamiliar with—millet, buckwheat, groats, garbanzo beans, lentils, brown rice, and tofu, to name a few. Remember, learning vegetarian cooking is probably far, far easier than you may imagine. Many beginners report enjoying cooking for the first time in their lives. An unexpected delight of vegetarian cooking is the fact that after learning a few basic principles (with a good cookbook as a guide) one can easily apply them to a seemingly endless number of grains, legumes, vegetables, and nuts. (And it is also extremely economical as well—a vegetarian diet can cut the average food bill by 50%).

If all else fails in your efforts to become a vegetarian, take an afternoon off and visit a slaughterhouse—this will be all the encouragement you need.

Any difficulty you may experience in making the transition in the beginning is not nearly as much as in quitting smoking, for instance. Most people find the immediate rewards (higher energy level, cleaner digestive system, increased mental clarity, sweeter body odor) so gratifying that the process of change becomes an exhilarating experience. The radiant health that results is not only physical; you will feel the joy of putting humanitarian ideals into action and the happiness that comes from performing a service of love to all the creatures (human and non-human) of this planet.

Eating a vegetarian diet, the natural diet for human beings, does the least harm to living creatures on our earth; and it helps us become more and more aware of the unity of life and realize the One Infinite Consciousness that underlies all.

PART II: FASTING

64

FASTING:
THE BODY'S NATURAL PURIFICATION PROCESS

Fasting is one of the most ancient cures of nature. Every animal instinctively fasts when it is sick; but we human beings have strayed so far from nature that often instead of obeying our instinctive lack of appetite when we are sick, and fasting to purify the body, we stuff it with more and more food, "to build up our strength." The ancient sages and spiritual teachers throughout the ages fasted often—not merely for health, but for mental and spiritual elevation, because as they said, "A full stomach does not like to think." The great Greek philosophers—Socrates, Plato, Pythagoras—always fasted before writing their works of philosophy or taking special examinations, because they knew that fasting stimulates mental power. The high priests of ancient Egypt also fasted for long periods of time. When the Greek philosopher and mathematician Pythagoras went to Egypt to study occult spiritual science, he had to first undergo a fast of 40 days, because the Egyptian masters explained, "Forty days is necessary in order that you may grasp what we will teach you." In the Bible we read again and again about fasting, for the early Jews and Christians used to fast not only to heal themselves but also to attain spiritual powers and a greater "closeness with God." Moses fasted for 40 days and 40 nights before he went up on Mt. Sinai to receive the 10 Commandments; and Jesus also fasted for 40 days, during which time he overcame all temptations and prepared himself for the great work and suffering he was to endure. In the Bible it is written: "When you fast, do not have a sad face but be clean and cheerful..." (Matthew 6:16-17). "Then (after the fast) shall thy light shine forth as the morning, and thy health shall spring forth speedily..." (Isaiah 58:8). The Buddha, too, often fasted to detach his mind from the physical world and attain higher consciousness, and after his longest fast, for 40 days, he attained enlightenment.

There are obviously great physical and mental benefits in fasting, which the ancient sages well knew, but modern people have forgotten. What are these benefits?

Stopping the intake of food for a limited period of time allows the body to clean itself and eliminate its accumulated poisons. Also, because no energy is being used in digestion, much extra energy is released to the brain for higher mental processes, such as deep meditation.

Disease from the accumulation of internal poisons

As we have seen, by eating too much acid-producing food (meats, refined foods such as white rice, white bread and white sugar, sweets, oily and fried foods, too much protein, etc.)—and especially by overeating—the body becomes over-acidic and many diseases result. As one nutrition expert says, "No animal on earth is so full of undigested, fermented and decayed foodstuffs from over-eating and unnatural food as the so-called civilized man." All the chemicals in our foods which are added to preserve, color, and flavor them; the noxious air pollution that suffocates our cities; drinking and smoking; the array of medications that modern humans have become dependent on; and especially debilitating emotional tensions which produce dramatic endocrine changes—all of these add chemical poisons to our system. Some of these poisonous waste products are passed off by the kidneys and bowels, or through the skin during perspiration. But many poisons cling to the cells, the organs, the glands, the arteries and veins, and flow in the bloodstream. These are more difficult to remove.

Doctors agree that this accumulation of poisons within the body is the main cause of disease, and not nasty "germs" from outside. Bacteria and viruses can only affect us when our bodies are already too weak from excessive impurities to resist them. Germs and viruses are in the air all around us every moment, in the food we eat, and inside our bodies; we succumb to them only when our systems give them a chance to grow and reproduce inside us. Thus even though many persons may be exposed to the same disease-carrying germs, only some people get the disease. Nutritionist Dr. Leon Patrick says, "When internal waste products or poisons remain in the body, we have the condition of toxemia—internal poisoning. Since toxemia is the presence of an excess amount of metabolic waste, it has been designated as the universal cause of all diseases."

Disease is the effort of the body to eliminate the waste, mucus and poisons which are clogging it and hindering its normal functions. Not the disease, but the body itself must be healed by cleansing it of all the accumulated poisons.

Early symptoms that the body is impure and susceptible to disease are: waking up in the morning with much mucus in the nose and throat, a stuffy or runny nose, sallow skin color, nervous irritability, a coated tongue, bad breath, offensive body odor, dizziness, gas, headaches, a feeling of heaviness of the stomach, poor appetite, bloodshot eyes, excess perspiration, etc. If you suffer from any of the above conditions, you should realize that this is nature's warning signal to purify your body at once. Doctors have stated that prolonged internal poisoning may lead to "faulty mental powers, severe headaches and backaches, declining vision, nervous tremors, extreme tiredness, muscular aches, ringing in the ears, hacking coughs and unusual sensitivity to dust."

Some common ailments caused by internal toxins are:

SKIN ERUPTIONS
The blood tries to eliminate the poisons through the skin, where they accumulate to form pimples, sores, boils, etc.

GAS
Dr. Irwin Kross says, "The putrified mass of undigested food in the intestines forms smelly gases which are partly absorbed into the bloodstream, causing more poisoning. Hemorrhoids are often caused by continual giving off of gases. These gases also back up from the intestines into the stomach, causing belching and distending the stomach and intestines. They also rise into the mouth and cause a bad odor and sour taste."

CONSTIPATION
As we have seen, constipation, the clogging of the intestines with poisonous waste products of the body, is one of the main causes of disease. In this condition the entire intestinal lining becomes covered with a slimy mucus which slows up the secretion of digestive fluids and reduces digestive power; this is called catarrh. As more and more waste is added, it becomes solidified until the intestine becomes like a thick tube with only a small open channel in the center, through which the food must pass. One European doctor stated that 60% of all the corpses he examined in autopsies had foreign matter such as worms and decades-old stones inside,

and the inside walls, encrusted by old, hardened feces, resembled a filthy stovepipe. "Many colons I found were distended to twice their natural size with only a very small hole through the center—although these people had regular bowel movements daily! As I stood looking at these colons, I wonder that anyone can live a week, much less for years, with such a cesspool of death and contagion always within them. The absorption of the deadly poisons back into the circulation cannot help but cause all the contagious diseases. In fact, my experience during the past 10 years has proved, by the rapid recovery of all diseases after the colon was cleaned, that in the colon itself lies the basic cause of almost all human ailments."

Some people take laxatives to relieve their chronic constipation, but this only aggravates the problem. Some laxatives act by irritating the walls of the intestines; as a result the intestines try to eject this irritating substance quickly, and with it eliminate intestinal wastes as well. Repeated use of such laxatives weakens the intestinal walls so they cannot function without this violent laxative lashing. Other laxatives dehydrate the body by drawing water from other parts of the body into the intestines to dilute hardened wastes and create diarrhea. Still other types lubricate and coat the waste materials with a slick layer so they can slip through the intestines; but this interferes with digestion and also hinders the absorption of precious vitamins such as vitamins A, D and E. Under no circumstances should laxatives be used regularly, and be depended on to produce a bowel movement. The body must be returned to a state of purity and health so it can regularly eliminate its wastes by itself, naturally. One of the best ways is through fasting. After special fasting treatment, patients eliminated as much as 10-15 pounds of old fecal matter which had been clogging their bodies for years.

FEVER

Fever is the body's natural way to purify itself; as the white blood cells wage war on the poisons inside, the metabolism speeds up and the body becomes hot.

GALLSTONES AND KIDNEY STONES
These are crystallized poisons which have accumulated in the gall bladder and kidneys. They may be as tiny as a grain of sand or, in the gall bladder, as large as a goose egg.

WARTS
Warts are caused by accumulated wastes that become lodged in the tissues of the foot or hand.

ATHEROSCLEROSIS & HIGH BLOOD PRESSURE
When poisonous wastes and fatty substances adhere to the sides of the blood vessels, especially the tiny capillaries, and block the smooth flow of blood, the heart muscle has to work harder to pump blood through these constricted vessels; it becomes larger, and high blood pressure, blood clots, heart disease, heart attack, and strokes result. Also the kidneys and endocrine glands, in the effort to purify the body of poisons, secrete various chemical substances which raise the blood pressure. Early warning symptoms of high blood pressure are headache, dizziness, shortness of breath, heart palpitation, and perspiration.

MENTAL AND EMOTIONAL DISTURBANCES
A body overburdened with poisonous wastes cannot send sufficient oxygen and energy to the brain. In fact, the brain itself becomes saturated with toxic waste, and as a result the thinking becomes impaired. Mental sluggishness and emotional disturbances can in fact be caused by impurities accumulated in the brain. (Even serious mental diseases have been cured by fasting.)

ARTHRITIS
The adjoining ends of the bones in the joints are covered with cartilage, a soft elastic tissue that cushions the joints to reduce friction. When acid wastes accumulate in the fluid which lubricates the joints, they become swollen, the ends of the bones become rough and jagged, and the cartilage becomes dry and brittle. Gradually the secretion dries up completely and the bones rub against each other in the painful condition of arthritis.

ALLERGIES AND ASTHMA

The bronchial tubes within the lungs are like tree roots, branching off from the windpipe in finer and finer tubes, and ending in tiny air sacs in the lungs. Due to excess poisons in the body, especially acid wastes, the mucus membranes which line these tubes become laden with impurities and are irritated and inflamed. Then the bronchial glands become overactive, and mucus accumulates inside these tubes. To neutralize these poisonous wastes the body secretes the enzyme histamine; in large amounts, histamine may often trigger an allergic reaction—wheezing, coughing, sneezing, runny nose, watery eyes—as the patient tries to expel the excess waste.

Breathing any irritating substance may also cause a sudden allergic or asthmatic attack. The allergic reaction may also occur as a result of eating certain foods, insect bites, etc., causing eczema, pimples, boils, or hives, as the wastes try to find their outlet through the pores of the skin.

LIVER DISEASE

The liver is the body's filter, which neutralizes and removes all the poisons in the body. A sick liver is like a filter clogged with dirt; it cannot work efficiently to secrete enough bile to fully digest the fats in the diet. If the poison-laden bile enters the bloodstream it causes jaundice; or the poisons may harden and form gallstones in the gallbladder. The cancer specialist Dr. Max Gerson writes, "All the metabolic disorders we call gastritis, ulcer, inflammation of the esophagus, gallbladder, intestines, pancreas, rectum, etc. are only stages of a process starting with liver failure and hardening of the blood vessels, and resulting sometimes in cancer." (Since eating excessive fatty foods overburdens the liver with fatty wastes, many doctors recommend eliminating meat from the diet and adopting a vegetarian diet which is low in fat.)

TOOTH DECAY

Poisonous wastes in the body also cause tooth decay and other mouth disorders. These wastes dissolve the outer enamel structure of the teeth and destroy the inner teeth. The gradual degeneration of the gums ultimately results in the loss of teeth.

Drugs to treat diseases

Many people, at the first sign of sickness, run to the pharmacy and buy drugs and antibiotics to stop their sickness. Actually these drugs merely treat the symptoms of the disease but cannot eliminate the root cause—a waste-filled body. So the disease is suppressed but not cured, and the drugs themselves remain in the body, adding still more poisons to an already overladen system. Nutritionist Arnold Ehret says, "I learned through years of practical experience that drugs are never eliminated as is the waste from foods, but are stored up in the body for decades. Hundreds of cases have come under my observation where drugs taken 10, 20, 30, and even 40 years were expelled together with mucus by fasting."

THE NATURAL CURE: FASTING

When the entire digestive system is permeated with the chronic abuse of modern eating, with waste products from the continued inflow of unassimilable food, and may even be laboring to throw off these morbid wastes through germs, fever or skin eruptions—to bring about the transmutation of the entire being, the radical cleaning of the whole body must be begun. All the putrefying refuse which is clogging the system must be eliminated through the absolute emptiness of fasting. Only when the digestive system is empty and fasting can it devour the wastes, burn them up, and eliminate them through the bloodstream.

Internal housecleaning

The body is your house; it is also your machine, the vehicle which carries you about and does all your work. You regularly clean out your house and discard waste and accumulated junk; you regularly clean your car or motorcycle of dirt, or it becomes clogged and ceases to run. But did you ever stop to think about cleaning your own insides? The best way to cleanse the body internally is by fasting. No one would attempt to clean the water pipe system of a city, and wash all the clogged filters, until they had first turned the water supply off. Fasting is just this: turning off the constant stream of food into the body and giving the body a chance to cleanse itself automatically. When you fast, you force your body to work on and digest the excess accumulation of waste in the body and then excrete it, thus purifying the whole system.

Many people fear fasting; they think fasting means starving themselves. This is not at all true. Dr. Patrik answers, "Proper fasting is never harmful; indeed, it is often the only procedure that will conserve nerve energy and permit nature to rally her forces for the fight against disease." Actually the body has plenty of resources to nourish itself for a long time; an experienced faster can fast safely for a month or longer! As one doctor explained, "People don't realize that the chief obstacle to fasting is overcoming the ingrained cultural, social and psychological fears of going without food."

Take the example of a cold. The first organ to be affected by poisons in the body is the mucus membrane. It starts to produce excess mucus in an effort to throw off all the poisons—and you "catch cold." Everyone knows how much mucus comes out of the body during a cold, from blowing the nose and coughing; this is the body's natural effort at self cleansing. In previous days, when people lived closer to nature and followed its natural laws, a cold or flu was easy to cure; the patients instinctively obeyed their loss of appetite, drank mostly fruit juices, and rapidly recovered. They felt much better afterwards than before, because so many poisons of the body were eliminated with the mucus. Today, people are wrongly taught that a germ or virus is responsible, and not their own living habits. To cure their colds they eat more highly concentrated foods instead of fasting, thus adding more indigestible, poisonous waste to their bodies. Or they take drugs which add still more poisons into their system. As a result, colds and flu often become complicated by more serious diseases. Dr. Robert G. Jackson recommends eating only fruits or fruit juices for at least 2 days as soon as the first signs of a cold appear. He says, "It is a well-known fact that, although the body which is improperly fed is apt to catch cold and suffer from various catarrhal and inflammatory diseases of the mucus membrane of the respiratory tract, a person who fasts never catches cold. And colds and catarrhal and inflammatory diseases rapidly clear up during a fruit fast. Colds are a reaction by which the body seeks to rid its debris-burdened cells of their incumbering substances via the mucus membranes. This debris is always deposited in the tissues, because it is so in excess in the bloodstream that it cannot all be carried in solution in the blood. If you have a cold and continue to eat regular foods, the blood will not reabsorb any of the substances formerly deposited in the tissues and cells."

The universal remedy for disease

The ancients well knew the efficacy of fasting to prevent and cure all types of diseases. The Greek Hippocrates, the "Father of Medicine," who lived to the age of 90, wrote, "Everyone has a doctor in him; we just have to help him in his work. To eat when you are sick is to feed your sickness." And the great Greek philosopher Paracelsus, wrote, "Those who fast are in the hands of the inner physician." Lately many modern doctors as well have noticed the "general well-being of a person on a fast," and are recommending fasting to mobilize the body's natural defenses against disease. Some of the benefits of fasting noted by physicians:

Fasting gives your entire system (heart, stomach, intestines, kidneys, lungs, pancreas, liver, etc.) a chance to rest and regain strength, so it can work with greatly increased efficiency after the fast. The heart and blood vessels, especially, which no longer have to pump so much blood to the digestive system for the assimilation of food, receive a much-needed "vacation."

Fasting causes the breakdown and excretion of poisonous wastes clinging to all the organs and tissues of the body, and thus cleanses the entire body, enabling it to work at top efficiency.

Fasting rejuvenates the entire system and restores youth to all the cells, tissues, and blood vessels. It slows down the aging process and increases longevity.

Fasting helps to re-establish normal, balanced secretions of the glands and organs.

Fasting conserves energy and allows it to be re-channeled for higher mental and spiritual pursuits, such as deep meditation.

Fasting clears the mind, sharpens the senses, and improves the memory. The empty stomach no longer draws blood away from the brain for digestion, and so the brain receives extra blood and energy. As the poisonous waste clogging the brain is cleansed and removed, concentration and clear thinking are greatly enhanced. Many famous personalities who have to make frequent public speeches have a rule: "Fast before an important speech and eat later."

Fasting makes the skin look younger and more radiant, as the skin pores clean themselves of the products of toxins from eating too much fats and sweets. Pimples, acne, skin infections, etc. can all be relieved, and the skin becomes clear and rosy. The eyes become clear and sparkling, and pure beauty shines from within.

Fasting helps remove the urge to smoke and drink. Excessive eating strains the nerves, which then seek relaxation through cigarettes and alcohol. Fasting relaxes the nerves and thus eliminates these cravings.

Fasting burns up excess fat and reduces excess weight. By cleansing the digestive system, fasting creates a normal and healthy appetite and ends the compulsion to overeat. Those who regularly overeat unnaturally stretch their stomachs, which then demand more food to fill them. Fasting restores the distended stomach to its normal size, and the unnatural and harmful gluttony disappears.

By burning up and excreting unwanted materials, fasting can remove unnatural growths in the body. Many people have been cured of tumors, diseased tissues, sores, swellings, stones and other abnormal growths by fasting.

Periodic fasts prevent illness by keeping the body clean and functioning at maximum strength and efficiency. Doctors have found that fasting increases resistance to infection.

Fasting is "nature's tranquilizer"—by relaxing the nervous system and easing anxieties, it helps cure insomnia. Often insomnia is caused by heartburn and acid indigestion from overeating and eating the wrong food. After a fast, many insomniacs discover they are sleeping better than they have in years. And because the body operates more efficiently during and after a fast, people find they need to sleep less.

When the body is given the much-needed rest of fasting, and all its cells, tissues and organs are cleansed, it regenerates itself and all its functions, especially digestion, are improved. Those who fast regularly experience increased strength, vigor and energy, mental clarity and calm. Many people have discovered the tremendous benefits of fasting and found their lives totally transformed:

"In my opinion the biggest discovery of our time is the ability to make oneself younger—physically, mentally and spiritually—through rational fasting. I am 85 years old and proud of my agility.

I can easily do yoga exercises standing on my head—few people my age are able to do such exercise. I eat twice a day and never between meals. Every week I fast for 24 hours and 3 or 4 times a year for 7 to 10 days at a time. I believe a person can live for 120 years or more. People do not use their common sense when it comes to food and drink and ways of living; and then they die too soon, not living even half their potential age. Even animals, if no one interferes, can live very long. Human beings are the only exception. Wild animals know how to live by instinct, what to eat and drink. But people eat the food that is most difficult to digest and drink poisonous drinks. And then they wonder why they cannot live for 100 years. In our minds we are all craving to live longer, but in practice unfortunately we are making our lives shorter... I am in perfect health and feel energetic because I learned nature's laws and follow them. Fasting is the key to health; it purifies every cell in the body. I am sure that 99% of the sick people suffer because of improper nourishment. People simply do not understand that they litter the body by many unnatural foods, and, because of this, poisonous substances are collected in the body. If you are interested in being in good physical and mental health and in increasing vitality, start to work today with nature, not against her."

—Russian man who has been fasting more than 50 years

"By fasting, I have found perfect health, a new state of existence, and a feeling of purity and happiness, something unknown to most humans..."

—Upton Sinclair

"To refuse food and drink is more than a pleasure, it is the joy of the soul!"

—Leo Tolstoy

"Fasting is essential for people who live in the city and are constantly exposed to poisonous car exhausts, factory fumes, and other poisonous air pollutants."

—Dr. Yuri Kikelayev, director of the fasting unit of the Moscow Psychiatric Institute

"Fasting is probably the best self-disciplining practice I know."
—**Dr. Walter Bloom, Vice President of Georgia
Institute of Technology**

"I was a sick man for 20 years or more, and then, in 1960, I discovered fasting. I used to have at least one cold a month. I don't catch colds any more. My ulcer has gone away. Until I started to fast, I used to be angry at the world., irritated with my customers. Thanks to fasting my disposition is much improved, my business is much improved, and I feel and look much better. I owe my life to fasting."
—**New York shoe manufacturer**

"Experienced fasters claim that the average eater utilizes only 35% of what he eats, but the person who regularly fasts can use up to 85%. Animals, of course, routinely fast when they are hurt. I had several deep bruises that did not get better for 3 weeks. When I fasted, the injuries disappeared. I assume the body's building blocks could go to work on the injuries because they were not preoccupied with the digestive process."
—**American teacher**

"I regard fasting as more a spiritual experience than a physical experience. I started fasting to rid my body of excess weight, but I quickly realized that the fast is very beneficial for the mind. Fasting helps me see more keenly, achieve new thoughts, intensify my feelings. After a few days without eating, I experience a higher state of consciousness naturally. Fasting inspires a sense of inner discipline and a controlled mind. Insight into suffering and happiness comes during the fast. Once craving for food goes away, the mind and the body seem to stop craving things that lead to negative emotions like envy, jealousy, greed and overriding ambition."
—**Graduate student at Columbia University, New York**

"I know the great benefits I have received from fasting. Every week I do a 24-hour fast. In addition, I fast about seven days, 4 times a year. Over many years (I am now 85 years old), I have been following this schedule, and I have kept myself in a superior state of health. I have an unlimited amount of energy for work and play— I never get tired, never get that worn-out, exhausted feeling... By fasting, the mind becomes sharpened, and in tune with the gentle voice of nature. Fasting has made my inner mind alert. I know positively that my mind works better and better after each fast. You must be the master. You must control the entire body with the mind."

—Dr. Paul C. Bragg, author of *The Miracle of Fasting*

Fasting for spiritual elevation

Those who fast, as we have seen, liberate much extra energy from the body since little of their energy is being used for digestion during this time. This energy should be properly channeled and not wasted. Since the mind is extremely clear, this is the best time for meditation; the extra energy can be used to elevate the mind to higher and higher states of consciousness. In India the word for fasting is *upavas* which means "remaining near the Supreme Consciousness" because for thousands of years yogis have practiced fasting not just for the physical health benefits, but to elevate their minds to higher states of awareness. As we have seen, in the past, the great saints and sages of all countries attained wisdom and mental powers by long fasting. They well knew that fasting—when pure blood bathes the brain and gives it tremendous energy and strength—is the best time to devote oneself to higher mental and spiritual effort to obtain rapid progress.

HOW TO FAST

In previous ages people fasted for many days, sometimes as long as 30 or 40 days. But in those days, people lived closer to nature, ate purer foods, exercised more, and were less affected by nervous tension and anxiety; so their bodies were more strong and pure and able to endure long fasts. But many modern people are so over-loaded with impurities that they cannot sustain a long fast. Thus short and regular fasts are recommended to purify the body with a minimum of strain—a one-day fast (from sunrise to sunrise), twice a month on special days, according to the moon (see next section). During the fast, one should get plenty of exercise, walking briskly in the open air and breathing deeply, to stimulate the blood circulation and speed up the elimination of wastes.

The best way to fast is to take nothing at all, not even water. In this way the fast works most quickly and efficiently, squeezing out all the poisons from the body, like squeezing out a dirty sponge. As one nutritionist explains, "The less you drink, the more powerfully and effectively the fast works." There is another important reason for not drinking water, related to the moon's effect on the body (see next section).

Fasting should be taken up gradually, not suddenly and abruptly. The first time you fast, you may take fruits and milk. The next time only fruits or fruit juices. Then, only water; and finally nothing at all. In this way you will gradually and easily adjust to the fast.

Weak or very sick persons who cannot undertake a complete fast should do a "half-fast" after lunch, until the next morning; in this way they can fast 4 times a month. Or they may take citrus juice, milk and fruits, or green leafy vegetable soup. Children, pregnant women and nursing mothers should not fast.

Experiences during the fast

Those who fast will generally feel extra health and energy and increased mental clarity during the fast day. But at the beginning, when the body is still full of poisons which are starting to be excreted, fasting may cause some weakness. Actually, this is a sign that the fast is working!—that the poisons and waste matter which have clogged the body for so long are being dissolved into the blood and prepared for excretion. The tongue may become coated with a whitish color; this is the waste and bacteria being eliminated on the inside of the entire mucus membrane, from the intestines and stomach up to the tongue—another indication that the cleansing process is taking place. One may blame the weakness on the lack of food and start to eat to "feel strong" again: but this temptation to eat should be resisted, for it will negate all the good effects of the fast. Firm determination during a fast also greatly strengthens the will power.

78

> *"While fasting, the extra food should be given to the poor, and the extra water should be given to the plants."*
> —P. R. Sarkar

For the same reason as above, even those people who are not fasting often wake up in the morning feeling weak and miserable. They may not have any appetite, but they feel they need to eat a big breakfast so they will feel better again. This is because during the 10 or 12 hours since dinner the night before, the body has been cleansing itself to some extent, and the waste poisons are entering their bloodstream to be eliminated. As soon as they eat in the morning, this process of elimination is stopped. Some persons wake up in the middle of the night feeling uneasy, and have to eat in order to sleep again: in other words, they have to put food into their stomachs in order to stop the digestion of poisons accumulated there. These are all warning signals that it is time to give the body a good internal cleaning.

After several fasts, the body will be purified and these feelings of weakness will disappear. There will probably not be any hunger at all; for since no sugar or starches are being ingested, the pancreas is at rest, and hunger pangs are reduced. One will feel stronger and better than ever before, with the capacity to think and work actively greatly increased instead of diminished. A British runner ran a 52-mile marathon with his stomach completely empty after a 24-hour fast—and he ran half an hour faster than his previous record!

And Dr. Anton Carlson, professor of physiology at the University of Chicago, discovered that a fast of three or four days before a basketball game usually increased the energy and endurance of the players!

How to break the fast

How to break the fast is almost as important as the fast itself. After you have cleansed and rested your entire system, if you stuff huge amounts of heavy foods back into your body, overloading and stretching your stomach again, you will negate all the good effects of the fast. It is thus recommended to break the fast the next morning after sunrise with a glass of lemon juice (about 1/4 of a fresh lemon in a glass of water), with a little salt or honey. Lemon juice is highly alkaline and is one of the most effective body cleansers. It neutralizes the acids and thins the mucus, all of which have been cleansed from the tissues during the fast, dissolving them so they can be easily excreted. Then eat 1/2 or a whole banana slowly, biting off small pieces and swallowing them whole without chewing. The banana acts as a sponge to absorb and neutralize the poisons in the stomach and intestines so they can be easily excreted; and it also lubricates the intestines for a smooth digestion. If possible, wait a 1/2 hour and then eat your breakfast.

The first meal after the fast should be light, with plenty of fruits or fresh vegetables (especially green leafy vegetables or sprouts) to loosen, dissolve, and wash out the remaining poisons from the digestive system. The fibrous vegetables act as a broom, and the fruits provide the water, to help you really sweep your digestive tract clean. The more easily digestible the breakfast, the more efficiently and quickly it will carry out the mucus and poisonous wastes from the stomach and intestines.

The day after the fast, take a good bath using a loofa sponge to wash off all the poisons that have been eliminated through the pores of the skin.

Everyone can and should fast

Some people think that only fat people can afford to fast, because they have extra fat to burn off during the fast, and that thin people cannot afford to lose any flesh. This is not at all the case. When you fast you are not burning your flesh but the useless and disease-carrying poisonous wastes in the body, and everyone can afford to lose these! As Dr. Ehret says, "Some people believe that the human engine cannot run a minute without solid food, protein and fat. Actually, the cleaner you are, the easier it is to fast. In other words, in a body free from all waste and poisons, when no solid foods are taken, the human body functions for the first time in its life without obstruction. The entire system works with an entirely different efficiency than ever before... Your brain will function in a manner that will surprise you, and for the first time in your life you will awaken to a real self-consciousness. Your soul will shout for joy and triumph over all misery in life. For the first time you will feel a vibration of vitality that shakes you delightfully. You will then realize that fasting is one of the keys to a superior life, and to the spiritual world."

FASTING AND THE MOON

The best days to fast are three days before the new moon and full moon.* Why these particular days? Because just as the moon has a great effect on the waters of this earth, it also has a great effect on our bodies and minds. As the moon's gravitational attraction causes tides in the ocean during the new and full moon periods, so it also causes "tides" in our bodies, which are over 70% water.

For many thousands of years people have realized the great effect of the new and full moons on human life. Primitive people worshipped the moon at these times, and held great feasts and rituals accompanied by frenzied dancing. Many omens and supernatural events have also been associated with these days, and even today there are many farmers all over the world who will only plant certain crops when the moon is full.

Recently scientists have taken an interest in the tremendous effect that the moon, especially the full and new moons have on our bodies and minds. According to scientific research, on these full and new moon days, and three days before and after, the moon's gravitational attraction draws the liquid in our bodies upwards into our brain. This excess of fluid in the brain disturbs its functioning, resulting in various mental and physical symptoms such as restlessness, irritability, extreme emotionalism, anger, and strange behavior.

Newspaper offices keep a calendar prominently posted on the wall, with the full moon dates circled in red because, as many editors have realized, during those days the most crimes occur, and so more reporters are needed on those shifts. Extra policemen are on duty at these times also, because more people tend to drink excessively, fight with their families and neighbors, and disturb the police with imaginary complaints and confessions. One police station reports, "Regularly each month on the full moon, a well-dressed retired man who is lovingly cared for by his children, lodges a complaint that they have been stealing from him. Another man misplaces his bicycle during that 3-day period, reports it stolen, and then finds it on the fourth day," Every full moon, a beautiful

*If for some pressing reason you cannot fast on these exact days, then fast the day before or after.

woman comes to the police station to curse the officers with abusive language. They endure her tirade silently until she runs out of breath and leaves. She causes no more trouble until the next full moon. One man always starts to direct traffic from the middle of the street alongside the traffic policeman. Fights start in many houses and bars. People come into the police station complaining that people are trying to kill them, or persecute them with "poison gas," "invisible rays," and "x-ray machines."

Mental hospitals, too, have to hire more attendants to control the patients during those days because they become extremely restless and often violent. One psychiatrist says, "I used to walk through the wards at night and notice a certain degree of stirring—what seemed to be a little emotional upheaval among the patients. Automatically I would look to see if the moon was full, and usually it was... During those three days there definitely was a certain irritation, tension, and restlessness among them." The ancient Romans well knew that madness if often caused by the moon; *lunacy* comes from the Latin word *luna*, or *moon*.

One prosperous businessman knows from experience that he is going to be very irritable during these days, and always warns his wife. Although he tries hard to control himself, he often becomes angry. His wife remarked, "Every time this full-moon period is over, I say to myself that I just should have been smarter and kept my mouth shut. I know the things I say during this time are going to upset him, although the same things wouldn't bother him at any other time in the month."

Controlling the mind; fasting without water

To control this very powerful and disturbing effect of the moon on our temperaments we must reduce the amount of excess fluid in the brain. Doctors know that if any part of the body is *edematous* or swollen with excess fluid, the best way to decrease the fluid in this part is to decrease the amount of fluid in the whole body, and then the excess fluid in that particular part will be automatically drawn out of that area by osmotic pressure, to supply the deficiency in other parts. So if there is edema or too much fluid in the brain as a result of stroke or accident, doctors inject a certain chemical into the body which quickly dehydrates it. Soon the excess fluid in the brain flows down into the body to provide the rest of the cells the liquid they need.

Instead of powerful chemicals, the natural way to balance the fluid in the body is to fast without water. This decreases the fluid in the whole body and thus the liquid from the brain is drawn down into the body's cells, and the disturbing effect of too much fluid in the brain is removed. (Also, as we have seen, fasting without water is the quickest and most effective way to cleanse the body of its poisons.)

But why fast on the third day before the new and full moons— why not fast on the new and full moon days themselves? Because, as we have seen, scientists have found that the emotional disturbance starts three days before, so we must counteract this effect from the very beginning, before it has a chance to greatly upset our bodies and minds. Recent discoveries by British scientists have shown that there are two days during the month when the electromagnetic vibration of the body radically changes—three days before the new and full moons. On these two days during the month there is a marked difference in the electrical potential, between the body's electromagnetic vibration at the navel and in the brain. Scientists are puzzled as to why these two particular days should manifest such changes—but yoga master have long understood the significance of these days* and regularly fasted at these times.

Even though many people during these periods may become irritable, restless and upset, those who fast without water will find that their minds remain balanced and calm.

Fasting to control our desires

According to yoga, the most vital fluid of the body is the lymph, which purifies the blood, helps in the secretion of hormones, and feeds and strengthens the brain. After supplying the brain, the remaining lymph is used to form spermatozoa and egg cells. For the proper development of the body and mind, adequate lymph is necessary, and a deficiency of lymph causes disease or mental dullness. But excess lymph is also harmful to the body; in all aspects of life, moderation is the rule of nature. If there is too much lymph in the body, then the sexual organs and glands are over-stimulated; this results in an excess of sexual desire which disturbs both body

---

* Called *Ekadashi* in Sanskrit, meaning eleven days after the full and new moons.

and mind. So for the purity and control of the mind, it is necessary to prevent the formation of excess lymph in the body by fasting 2 days a month. By eating 28 days a month the body obtains enough food to produce just the right amount of lymph, not too much, and in this way the purity of the body and the balance and peace of the mind can be maintained.

CONCLUSION

The goal of yoga is the perfection of the individual and the gradual expansion of one's consciousness into higher and higher states of awareness until ultimately it merges in the Infinite. For this expansion, there must be a parallelism in all aspects of life—between the physical and mental, and between the mental and spiritual. When all the layers of our being are in harmony, we remain in a state of health and vitality, peace and bliss.

Eating the proper foods and fasting regularly not only purifies the vehicles for our journey to higher consciousness—our bodies—making them free from disease, light, youthful and full of energy, but also keeps our emotions balanced and our minds serene and calm.

Try a vegetarian diet—the original food and future diet of all humanity—and fast regularly, and start to experience the profound transformation in your body, mind and spirit—from today.

"The following are the 6 secrets to attain longevity:
1. Proper physical exercise.
2. Taking meals only on the urge of appetite.
3. Going to bed as soon as sleep comes on.
4. Regular spiritual practices.
5. Fasting at intervals.
6. Half-bath before sleep and spiritual practices."
—P.R. Sarkar

TABLES OF FOOD COMPOSITION

FOOD	Approx. measure	Weight grams	Calories	Protein grams	Carbo-hydrate grams	Fiber grams	gra
DAIRY PRODUCTS							
Cow's milk, whole	1 qt.	976	660	32	48	0	
skim	1 qt.	984	360	36	52	0	
Buttermilk, cultured	1 cup	246	127	9	13	0	
skim, non-instant (powdered milk)	2/3 cup	85	290	30	42	0	
Yogurt, of partially skim milk	1 cup	250	120	8	13	0	
Ice cream, commercial	1 cup	188	300	6	29	0	
Cheese, cottage	1 cup	225	240	30	6	0	
Cheddar, grated	1/2 cup	56	226	14	1	0	
Cream cheese	1 oz.	28	105	2	1	0	
OILS, FATS & SHORTENINGS							
Butter	1 T.	14	100	t	t	0	
Oils							
Corn, soy, peanut cottonseed	1 T.	14	125	0	0	0	
Olive	1 T.	14	125	0	0	0	
Safflower, sunflower seed, walnut	1 T.	14	125	0	0	0	
VEGETABLES							
Artichoke, globe	1 large	100	8-44	2	10*	2	
Asparagus, green	6 spears	96	18	1	3	.5	
Beans, green snap	1 cup	125	25	1	6	.6	
Lima, green	1 cup	160	140	8	24	3	
Bean sprouts, uncooked	1 cup	50	17	1	3	.3	
Beet greens, steamed	1 cup	100	27	2	6	1.4	
Beetroots, boiled	1 cup	165	68	1	12	.8	
Broccoli, steamed	1 cup	150	45	5	8	1.9	
Brussels sprouts, steamed	1 cup	130	60	6	12	1.7	
Cabbage, steamed	1 cup	170	40	2	9	1.3	
Carrots							
Cooked, diced	1 cup	150	45	1	10	.9	
Raw, grated	1 cup	110	45	1	10	1.2	
Cauliflower, steamed	1 cup	120	30	3	6	1	
Celery, cooked, diced	1 cup	100	20	1	4	1	

t Indicates trace only.   *Largely Inulin.   **richest source of arachidonic acid.

	MINERALS				VITAMINS				
Iron mg.	Calcium mg.	Phos. mg.	Potass. mg.	Sodium mg.	A units	B1 mg.	B2 mg.	Niacin mg.	C mg.
.4	1,100	930	210	75	1,560	.32	1.7	.8	6
.4	1,192	940	215	78	0	.4	1.7	.8	6
.1	298	270	52	19	180	.1	.4	.2	2
.4	1,040	940	210	75	t	.2	1.4	.7	t
.1	295	270	50	19	170	.1	.4	.2	t
.1	175	150	170	140	740	18	.3	.1	t
.9	207	360	170	625	430	.1	.6	.2	0
.6	435	390	90	540	700	t	.2	t	0
.1	18	170	25	180	440	t	t	1	0
t	3	0	4	120	460	0	**	0	0
0	0	0	0	0	0	0	0	0	0
0	0	0	0	0	0	0	0	0	0
0	0	0	0	0	0	0	0	0	0
1.3	50	69	300	30	150	t	t	.7	8
1.7	18	43	130	3	700	t	t	.9	18
.9	45	20	204	2	830	t	.1	.6	18
2.5	44	105	320	2	290	.2	.1	1.9	15
3.8	19	170	514	3	40	.2	.1	1.3	t
3.2	118	45	332	76	5,100	t	.1	.3	30
1	24	44	324	64	30	t	t	.5	10
2.1	190	100	405	15	5,100	t	.2	1.2	105
1.7	44	95	400	14	520	t	.1	.6	60
.8	78	50	240	23	150	t	t	.3	56
.9	38	55	600	75	18,130	t	t	.7	6
.9	43	29	410	51	13,000	t	t	.7	7
1.2	26	84	220	11	100	t	.1	.6	34
.5	54	40	300	80	0	t	t	.4	7

SOURCE: U.S. Department of Agriculture, Agriculture Handbook No. 8.

86

FOOD	Approx. measure	Weight grams	Calories	Protein grams	Carbo- hydrate grams	Fiber grams	gra
Collards, steamed leaves	1 cup	150	51	5	8	2	
Corn, steamed	1 ear	100	92	3	21	.8	
Cucumbers, 1/8" slices	6	50	6	t	1	.2	
Dandelion greens, steamed	1 cup	180	80	5	16	3.2	
Eggplant, steamed	1 cup	180	30	2	9	1.2	
Kale, steamed	1 cup	110	45	4	8	.9	
Kohlrabi, raw, sliced	1 cup	140	40	2	9	1.5	
Lentils	1 cup	200	212	15	38	2.4	
Lettuce, loose leaf, green	1/4 head	100	14	1	2	.5	
Okra, diced, steamed	1,1/3cups	100	32	1	7	1	
Parsley, chopped, raw	2T.	7	2	t	t	t	
Parsnips, steamed	1 cup	155	95	2	22	3	
Peas, fresh, steamed	1 cup	100	70	5	12	2.2	
split, cooked	1/2 cup	100	115	8	21	.4	
Peppers, green	1 large	100	25	1	6	1.4	
Potatoes, baked	1 med.	100	100	2	22	.5	
French-fried	10pieces	60	155	1	20	.4	
Potato Chips	10	20	110	1	10	t	
Radishes, raw	5 small	50	10	t	2	.3	
Rutabagas, diced	2/3 cup	100	32	t	8	1.4	
Soybeans, unseasoned	1 cup	200	260	22	20	3.2	
Spinach, steamed	1 cup	100	26	3	3	1	
Squash	1 cup	210	35	1	8	.6	
Sweet potatoes, baked	1 med.	110	155	2	36	1	
Tomatoes, Raw, 2 by 21/2	1 med.	150	30	1	6	.6	
Turnip greens, steamed	1 cup	145	45	4	8	1.8	
Turnips, steamed, sliced	1 cup	155	40	1	9	1.8	
Watercress, leaves & stems, raw	1 cup	50	9	1	1	.3	

FRUITS

FOOD	Approx. measure	Weight grams	Calories	Protein grams	Carbo- hydrate grams	Fiber grams	gra
Apple Juice	1 cup	250	125	t	34		
Apple vinegar	1/3 cup	100	14	t	3	0	
Apples, raw	1 med.	130	70	t	18	1	
Apricots Dried, uncooked	1/2 cup	75	220	4	50	1	
Fresh	3 med.	114	55	1	14	.7	

MINERALS					VITAMINS				
Iron mg.	Calcium mg.	Phos. mg.	Potass. mg.	Sodium mg.	A units	B1 mg.	B2 mg.	Niacin mg.	C mg.
1.2	282	75	393	40	11,700	t	.2	1.5	55
.5	4	120	300	t	300	t	t	1.1	12
.1	5	9	80	3	0	t	t	.1	4
5.6	337	126	760	130	27,300	.3	.2	1.3	29
.9	17	60	390	2	10	t	t	.3	8
1.3	130	57	260	29	8,000	t	.2	.3	60
.8	66	70	520	10	t	t	t	.5	85
4.1	50	238	505	15	40	t	t	1.6	0
2	35	26	260	9	1,900	t	t	.8	18
.7	82	62	370	1	700	t	t	.8	20
.4	14	7	80	1	580	t	t	.2	14
1.1	88	120	570	11	0	t	.2	.3	19
1.9	22	122	290	1	950	.3	.1	2.3	24
1.7	11	89	296	13	40	.2	t	.9	0
.4	11	25	170	t	370	t	t	.8	120
.7	13	66	500	4	10	.1	t	1.2	15
.7	9	6	510	6	0	t	t	1.8	8
.4	6	38	210	200	t	t	t	.6	0
.5	5	53	130	4	15	t	t	.1	12
.4	40	35	170	4	350	t	t	.7	21
5.4	150	360	1,080	4	60	.4	.1	1.2	0
.2	124	33	470	74	11,800	.1	.2	.6	30
.8	8	32	480	8	700	t	.1	1.3	24
1	36	58	300	12	8,900	.1	t	.7	24
.9	16	40	360	5	2,600	t	t	.8	70
3.5	375	75	—	—	15,300	.1	.6	1	90
.8	62	51	345	87	t	t	t	.6	28
.8	75	27	140	25	2,500	t	1	.4	80
1.2	15	12	200	5	90	t	t	8	8
.6	6	9	100	1	0	0	0	0	0
.4	8	13	130	1	50	t	t	t	3
4.1	50	75	780	19	8,000	t	.1	3	9
.5	18	30	280	1	2,900	t	t	.7	10

FOOD	Approx. measure	Weight grams	Calories	Protein grams	Carbo-hydrate grams	Fiber grams	Fa gram
Nectar, or juice	1 cup	250	140	1	36	2	
Avocado	1/2	108	185	2	6	1.8	1
Banana	large	150	85	1	23	.9	
Blackberies, fresh	1 cup	144	85	2	19	6.6	
Cantaloupe	1/2 med.	380	40	1	9	2.2	
Cherries, fesh, raw	1 cup	114	65	1	15	.3	
Dates, dried	1 cup	178	505	4	134	3.6	
Figs, dried, large, 2 by 1"	2	42	120	2	30	1.9	
Fresh, raw	3 med.	114	90	2	22	1	
Grapefruit, fresh, 5" diameter	1/2	285	50	1	14	1	
Grapefruit juice	1 cup	250	100	1	24	1	
Grapes	1 cup	160	100	1	26	.7	
Lemon juice, fresh	11/2 cup	125	30	t	10	t	
Oranges, fresh, 3' diameter	1 med.	180	60	2	16	1	
Orange juice, fresh	8 Oz.	250	112	2	25	.2	
Papaya, fresh	1/2 med.	200	75	1	18	1.8	
Peaches, fresh, raw	1 med.	114	35	1	10	.6	
Pears, raw, 3 by 21/2"	1 med.	182	100	1	25	2	
Persimmons, Japanese	1 med.	125	75	1	20	2	
Pineapple, raw diced	1 cup	140	75	1	19	.6	
Plums, raw, 2" diam.	1	60	30	t	7	.2	
Prunes, cooked	1 cup	270	300	3	81	.8	
Raisins, dried	1/2 cup	80	230	2	62	.7	
Raspberries, raw, red	3/4 cup	100	57	t	14	5	
Rhubarb, cooked & sweetened	1 cup	270	385	1	98	1.9	
Strawberries, raw	1 cup	149	54	t	12	1.9	
Tangerines, fresh	1 med.	114	40	1	10	1	
Watermelon, 4 by 8"	1 wedge	925	120	2	29	3.6	

BREADS, CEREALS, GRAINS AND GRAIN PRODUCTS

FOOD	Approx. measure	Weight grams	Calories	Protein grams	Carbo-hydrate grams	Fiber grams	Fa gram
Biscuits, 2 1/2" diams.	1	38	130	3	18	t	
Bread, cracked wheat	1 slice	23	60	2	12	.1	
Rye	1 slice	23	55	2	12	.1	
White	1lb. loaf	454	1,225	39	229	9	1
Whole wheat	1lb. loaf	454	1,100	48	216	67.5	1
Corn meal, yellow	1 cup	118	360	9	74	1.6	
Crackers, graham	2 med.	14	55	1	10	t	

MINERALS					VITAMINS				
Iron mg.	Calcium mg.	Phos. mg.	Potass. mg.	Sodium mg.	A units	B1 mg.	B2 mg.	Niacin mg.	C mg.
.5	22	30	440	t	2,300	t	t	.5	7
.6	11	42	600	4	310	.1	.2	1.7	15
.7	8	44	390	1	190	t	t	.7	10
1.3	46	46	220	t	290	t	t	.5	30
.8	33	64	910	40	6,000	t	t	1	50
.4	18	20	270	1	620	t	t	.4	10
5.7	105	110	1,300	1	100	.1	.2	3.9	0
1.7	80	55	390	15	40	.1	t	.3	0
.4	35	20	110	1	90	t	t	.6	3
.5	21	54	290	4	10	t	t	.3	72
1	20	40	280	2	20	t	t	.4	84
.6	18	30	240	6	120	t	t	.4	7
.2	8	13	80	4	20	t	t	.1	50
.5	50	40	300	t	240	1	t	.3	75
.5	27	42	500	2	500	2	t	1	129
.5	40	32	470	6	3,500	t	t	.6	8
.5	9	22	31	5	1,320*	t	t	1	7
.5	13	29	182	3	30	t	t	.2	7
.4	7	28	310	1	2,710	t	t	.2	11
.4	22	12	210	1	180	.1	t	.3	83
.3	10	10	100	t	200	t	t	.3	3
4.5	60	100	810	10	1,800	t	.2	1.8	3
2.8	50	112	575	19	15	.1	t	.4	0
.9	40	37	190	t	130	t	t	.3	24
1.1	112	39	510	15	70	t	0	.2	17
1.2	20	24	157	2	50	t	t	.5	59
.4	33	23	110	2	420	t	t	.2	39
1.2	63	96	600	2	520	t	t	.2	8
.7	61	58	40	208	0	t	t	.7	0
.4	16	25	50	125	0	t	t	.3	0
.4	17	29	52	120	0	t	t	.3	0
10.9	318	662	720	2,655	0	1.1	.7	10.4	0
10.4	449	1,083	810	2,880	0	1.2	1	12.9	0
1.8	6	178	284	1	500	.4	—	2	3
.3	3	56	45	90	0	t	t	.3	9

* If yellow only.   — No data Available.

FOOD	Approx. measure	Weight grams	Calories	Protein grams	Carbo-hydrate grams	Fiber grams	gra
soda, 2 1/2"square	2	11	45	1	8	t	
Farina	1 cup	238	105	3	22	0	
Flour, soy, full fat	1 cup	110	460	39	33	2.9	
Wheat, whole	1 cup	120	390	13	79	2.8	
Macaroni, cooked	1 cup	140	155	5	32	.1	
Noodles	1 cup	160	200	7	37	.1	
Oatmeal, or rolled oats	1 cup	236	150	5	26	4.6	
Pancakes Wheat, refined flour, 4" diam.	4	108	250	7	28	.1	
Pizza, cheese, 1/8 of 14" diam	1 slice	75	180	8	23	t	
Popcorn, with oil and salt	2 cups	28	152	3	20	.6	
Puffed rice	1 cup	14	55	t	12	t	
Rice, brown	1 cup	208	748	15	154	1.2	
Converted	1 cup	187	677	14	142	.4	
White	1 cup	191	692	14	150	.3	
Rice, polish	1/2 cup	50	132	6	28	1.2	
Spaghetti with tomatoes and cheese	1 cup	250	210	6	36	.5	
Wheat germ	1 cup	68	245	17	34	2.5	
Wheat cereal, unrefined	1/4 cup	30	103	4	25	.7	

DESSERTS & SWEETS

FOOD	Approx. measure	Weight grams	Calories	Protein grams	Carbo-hydrate grams	Fiber grams	gra
Honey, strained	2 T.	42	120	t	30	0	
Jams, marmalades, preserves	1 T.	20	55	0	14	t	
Molasses, blackstrap	1 T.	20	45	0	11	0	
Cane, refined	1 T.	20	50	0	13	0	
Sugar, beet or cane	1 cup	200	770	0	199	0	
Brown, firm-packed, dark	1 cup	220	815	0	210	0	
Syrup, maple	2 T.	40	100	0	25	0	

MINERALS					VITAMINS				
Iron mg.	Calcium mg.	Phos. mg.	Potass. mg.	Sodium mg.	A units	B1 mg.	B2 mg.	Niacin mg.	C mg.
.1	2	19	12	110	0	t	t	.3	9
.8	31	29	20	33	0	.1	t	1	9
88	218	613	1,826	1	121	.9	.2	2.3	0
3.9	49	464	445	3	0	.6	.2	.2	59
.6	11	82	276	1	0	t	t	.4	9
1	16	52	—	—	60	t	t	.8	9
1.7	21	140	142	508	0	.2	t	.4	0
1.3	158	159	135	470	110	.1	.1	.9	5
.7	157	147	96	525	570	1	.1	.8	9
.8	4	90	—	646	0	t	t	.7	9
.3	2	82	57	t	0	t	t	.4	0
4	78	608	310	18	0	.6	.1	9.2	0
1.6	53	244	300	6	0	.3	t	7.6	0
1.6	46	258	247	4	0	t	t	1.8	0
8	35	553	357	t	0	.9	.2	14	0
2	45	135	407	955	830	t	t	1	19
5.5	57	744	550	5	0	1.4	.5	3.1	0
1.1	15	130	126	1	0	.2	.1	1.4	0
.4	2	2	22	2	0	t	t	t	2
.1	14	t	19	3	t	t	t	t	1
2.3	116	14	585	19	0	t	t	t	0
.9	30	9	185	3	0	0	0	0	0
0	0	0	0	0	0	0	0	0	0
5.7	167	38	688	60	0	0	0	0	0
.6	41	3	70	4	0	t	t	t	0

FOOD	Approx. measure	Weight grams	Calories	Protein grams	Carbo- hydrate grams	Fiber grams	gra
NUTS, NUT PRODUCTS, AND SEEDS							
Almonds, dried	1/2 cup	70	425	13	13	1.8	
Brazil nuts, unsalted	1/2 cup	70	457	10	7	2	
Cashews, unsalted	1/2 cup	70	392	12	20	.9	
Coconut, shredded, sweetened	1/2 cup	50	274	1	26	2	
Peanut butter, natural	1/3 cup	50	284	13	8	.9	
Peanuts, roasted	1/3 cup	50	290	13	9	1.2	
Pecans, raw, halves	1/2 cup	52	343	5	7	1.1	
Sesame seeds, dry	1/2 cup	50	280	9	10	3.1	
Sunflower seeds	1/2 cup	50	280	12	10	1.9	
Walnuts, English, raw	1/2 cup	50	325	7	8	1	
BEVERAGES							
Carbonated colas	12 oz.	346	137	0	38	0	
Fruit-flavored soda	12 oz.	346	161	0	42	0	
SUPPLEMENTARY FOODS							
Powdered yeast, brewer's	1/4 cup	33	91	13	12	.6	

t indicates trace only
— No data available
* Add 200 mg for salted nuts.

		MINERALS				VITAMINS			
Iron mg.	Calcium mg.	Phos. mg.	Potass. mg.	Sodium mg.	A units	B1 mg.	B2 mg.	Niacin mg.	C mg.
3.3	163	353	541	2	0	.2	.6	2.4	0
2.3	124	464	476	1	t	.6	.1	1	0
2.9	29	242	325	40*	70	.3	.1	1.2	0
1	8	56	176	0	0	t	t	.4	1
1	30	204	337	2	0	.5	.1	7.9	0
1	37	200	337	2.2*	0	.2	.1	8.8	0
1.2	36	144	300	t*	60	.4	.1	.4	1
5.2	580	308	360	30	15	.4	.1	2.7	0
3.5	60	418	460	15	0	1.8	.2	13.6	0
1.5	50	190	225	1	15	.1	.1	4	1
0	0	—	—	—	0	0	0	0	0
0	0	—	—	—	0	0	0	0	0
5	70	584	631	40	t	5.2	1	12.9	0